TulipTree
review

SPRING/SUMMER 2021
issue #9

Wild Women

TULIPTREE
PUBLISHING, LLC

Copyright © 2021 TulipTree Publishing, LLC
Cañon City, Colorado
Publisher & Editor in Chief, Jennifer Top

ISBN: 978-1-7349690-3-0

www.tuliptreepub.com

Contents

The Girl Who Visited the Alligator Queen

Couri Johnson

You're nobody till somebody loves you,
You're nobody till somebody cares.
—Fucking Dean Martin

ON THE INTERSECTION OF MARKET, WITH ITS DRIED HUSKS OF WHAT WERE once family-owned businesses, the tattoo and pawn shops that followed, and its beer can littered devil strips, and Pinebrook, with its redbrick shopping plazas, its vegan options, and its smooth new sidewalks, sits the mall. Its exterior is lint gray, save for the ghostly white shadows left by long-gone store names. The doors and windows are boarded up, and the boards have all been tagged by artists of varying skill levels trying to tackle the same thematic elements and forms: magic mushrooms with swirling eyes and fat brown blunts hanging out of their slack mouths, nude women spreading their legs, or bending over, or headless and bound, and a litany of names telling the empty lot who'd been there and when and what they did and who with. But one set of doors, on the east end farthest away from the road, is unboarded. These doors are left untouched, unsprayed, unlocked. The frames of them are lined with fairy lights—pinks and purples and the kind of blues that become bruises wherever they fall. The lights lead from the door through the littered hallway and disappear around the corner by the pretzel kiosk where they hook to the left.

This is the path to the Alligator Queen and her court.

I came here first in October, when all the trees in the parking lot had stripped themselves down to skeletons and strewn their leaves across the cement. Every step I took had a crunch to it, like someone tearing sloppy and quick into a carrot. The kind of sound that anybody nearby would wince at, the kind of sound that could never go unnoticed.

NO ONE GOES TO the mall now. Well, not no one, but hardly anyone. And those that I have heard about going have always been women, and these have all been whispers, indirect retellings; I heard from my neighbor who heard from her coworker who knew a woman who met a woman at a bar who went and stood before the Alligator Queen and her court. And all the Alligator Queen's court is female, the stories say.

My coworker first told me about the Alligator Queen. I suppose because she was tired of me the way I was. The way I was always in a tizzy. I couldn't help that though. I had told her I couldn't help it. And so maybe she thought the Alligator Queen could.

But I didn't go to the Alligator Queen to help fix who I was. I went hoping she could help me fill up the hunger that made me that way. The symptom, I guess, and not the root.

HERE'S A STORY ABOUT me, to help you understand.

One time, I was in training for this job. I've trained for a lot of jobs. Almost all trainings are the same, I think, for most jobs. Or at least most jobs that I've done, I don't know about you. And I have a problem with sitting still at these things, you know, so I doodle to keep me from fidgeting. No one likes people who fidget all the time. At the end of the day, I would leave these trainings with notebook pages covered in tight spirals and pointed V's and cubes and eyeballs and telephones and little sets of butterfly wings without the bug part attached. There were a couple of us there to be trained all together, and then one woman up front in charge of us all.

There was another trainee who took against me, see, and I'm not sure why exactly but that's just how it was. I thought maybe I had known her from somewhere else, and I guess maybe I was suspicious of that to begin with. Maybe I didn't act like you should when you first meet someone, because I was never sure if I knew her from before or not, and if so, how and what did she know about me? A lot of times people just look like other people. If you meet enough people, you see a pattern in them, and how they're all just one big related thing, repeating. That's not my fault.

But she took against me.

On day three of the training, in the middle of the part about customer complaints, the woman who took against me snapped to the woman in charge that I wasn't paying attention.

"She isn't listening," she said. "She's drawing."

There was a moment where everyone went quiet and looked at me, and I sat looking at the pen in my hand and the half-finished lips on my paper. I could set the pen down and sit up straight, I figured, or I could keep drawing. There was a choice there I could make, and that choice would set me down one path or another to who knows where on either end. So, I sat there hunched with the pen still in my hand and the lips still unfinished, and my face red and hot like I'd just drank salsa right out of the bottle.

"What did I just say?" the woman in charge asked.

I looked from her, to the woman who took against me, back to the woman in charge, and then to my paper. "You said even if the customer is wrong, you must make the customer happy," I said. I'd heard this line many times in my life, maybe as many times as I've heard my own name.

You understand that that's a joke, don't you? But still, it's how it felt, really.

Anyway, that's what the woman in charge said, word for word, and I said it back word for word, so next she says, "That's right. Word for word."

And the tone in her voice made me set the pen down and look back up at her, and she was smiling at me, her eyes crinkled up at the ends, and her pupils were big saucers full of light, and the heat in my face was worse, but more pleasant.

So, said my thoughts.

"Some people have brains like that," she said to the room. "Busy-brains, brains that are running too quick, brains that can do—have to do—more things at a time than other brains. Like they've got two brains, really. And if you don't keep them both occupied, then they'll just trip over each other, each trying to win attention, to come out the victor in the end.

"So, I let her doodle," she finished, and her pupils weren't saucers, and her eyes weren't crinkled but narrowed, but it didn't matter, or rather, it mattered a great deal, because she wasn't looking at me, she was looking at the woman who took against me.

So, this is it, I'd thought. *Isn't it?*

I did very well at that job while I was working under her. Because of that look she gave me, those saucer eyes, and the way she spoke about me. That's all it takes, and then I am someone's. Not, you understand, in a sexual way. Sometimes it can end up like that, but that's more like a comorbidity that can occur or not occur, depending. I just want to have them see me in the repeating pattern of people, and then look closer, you understand?

After a month, she started training a new batch of employees, and I never got to see her anymore, or if I did, she was leading around a group of other people and talking to them. I had to leave that job, not long after that. Before I did, I stopped by her office, but she wasn't there. So instead I took one of the pens off her desk, and I left. Then I went to the job with the girl who told me about the Alligator Queen and her court, told me she couldn't take watching me fret with my phone, and reread texts, and unball and reball the same tattered napkin I kept in my purse.

* * *

BEYOND THE DOORS, THE sound of my steps didn't matter anymore. There were new sounds. Off in the distance, down so many turns that it was more like something that was playing in your head than a something that you were really hearing, there was music. Jaunty organs and wheezing accordions and beating drums and trilling pipes that didn't stumble or pause when their notes went sour but just kept rolling on. And underneath all that, rustles and slithers, above and behind and to my sides. The stories sometimes talk about these sounds—they'd tell you not to look, to keep your eyes straight ahead, that the people who looked were the ones who didn't come back. That there are people who go before the Alligator Queen that don't come back. That these people were ones who had broken some rule, and this is one of them; don't look, when you hear those rustles. Don't search out the source of the noise.

Sometimes I catch myself wondering if my coworker didn't want me to come back. But this isn't a good thing to wonder over, is it? But it happens, you understand, sometimes, those kinds of thoughts happen. It's about if you attend to them or not, and how.

Of course, I looked when I heard the sounds. Of course, I did.

ANOTHER RULE, AND THIS one is one that is always consistent, is this: you must come bearing a gift for the Alligator Queen. Not something stupid, either, like a gift card, or a fruit basket—the kind of gifts that accidently expose how little you know and care about someone. The gift has to be a real gift. It has to have value to it.

I brought my mother's ring.

THE PATH ENDS AT the food court, where the Alligator Queen conducts all her official business. They have the tables stacked into a rising pyramid, one on top of the other, where they sit based on their rank and importance.

Down on the ground, spread out on either side of the pyramid, is the band and the court jesters, wailing away on their instruments or doing rolls, and bouncing balls on the pointed tips of their noses, up and down and over and over. They're dressed in the tatters of colorful children's clothes, and they wear caps made from the decapitated heads of stuffed animals. On the first level sits the guard in long black dresses with necklaces made of silverware tied together with electrical wires around their neck. Then above them, the ladies-in-waiting, who have paint spread above the tips of their grins like rouge, who wear low-cut sequin gowns that hang down to show off the start of their soft bellies and the tangled brassieres that hang off their crooked arms. After that, it's the council, with their taped-on glasses, powdered wigs, and dark, silky bathrobes, who take up two rows, one of four and one of three. The council switches each day, who is on what level, to keep from fighting. They're all equal, and they know that, but that doesn't keep feelings from being hurt if they're sat too long on the lower level. And so, a system was put in place. There are systems that can keep that kind of thing from happening, says the Alligator Queen.

She is at the top, where there's two tables standing a table's length apart. The other was empty, the first time I came. The Alligator Queen lay alone across from it, naked and curled, tail twitching. But as I approached, she rose to her full height and everyone turned to me, and she said,

"Come here, child, and let me look at you."

HERE IS ANOTHER STORY for you to understand.

One time I was on the bus across from this boy who had those big, bulky headphones on. They were so loud that I could hear the music playing from all the way across the aisle. He had built himself a bubble, a strong bubble, and I thought, you see, that if I could get into that bubble it would be something quite special to do. And then it could be something where we shared it. An us bubble—safe, and outside of everybody else.

He caught me looking at him and he popped one off his ear, and we got off at the same stop together. Then we got to his house and the headphones came off completely, and I thought *so.*

So, why not?

I lay next to him and my mind went *so, so, so,* his hands over my ears like speakers broadcasting back my thoughts and pulse. When he was firmly asleep, I made my way around his room. I stopped at the desk and fingered the headphones. Picked them up and felt the weight of them. I wanted to dismantle them and put one on my ear, and the other on his, and then press our free ears together to become one continuous cave of noise.

Instead, I picked up his half-finished pack of gum and put it inside my sock. Then I lay back down next to him, and put my ear close to his, and thought *so.*

So, this is it, isn't it?

But the next day, when we were walking to the bus, the headphones went back on and I could feel, really feel, the surface of the bubble between us when I tried to take his hand. It was like glass, smooth and unyielding with nothing to grab onto and no way in.

I put the gum in my desk drawer and started walking everywhere after that.

THE ALLIGATOR QUEEN PUT a telescope to her eye so she could watch me picking at the fingers on my right hand with my left, surrounded by the jesters.

"What is it that you want?" she asked me, after a long time.

I pulled my thumb, I pulled my index, I pulled my middle finger, and looked down at my feet.

"To be seen," I said. "To be loved."

Laughter rustled its way down from the council to the ladies-in-waiting to the guard to the ground floor that sounded like a breeze had kicked up a storm of leaves. Only the Alligator Queen didn't laugh, but kept her telescope aimed at me.

"You have asked for two things," the Alligator Queen said. "And two very different things at that. Have you brought two gifts?"

"Are they that different?" I asked. More laughter rustled; more fingers got pulled.

"They're like the sun and the moon," the Alligator Queen said. "Sure, they can come together, but only on rare occasions. So, have you brought two gifts?"

"No, I've only got the one," I said.

"Well, then choose," said the Alligator Queen.

Eventually the ladies-in-waiting began to fidget with their bra straps, and the council tapped their claws against the tables, and one of the musicians started tuning her mandolin.

"Hurry up, girl," one of the councilwomen said.

"Let her take her time," the Alligator Queen said, but we were all fidgeting, and no one likes that, so I said,

"The last one then. Love, I guess."

"From whom?"

"Well, there's this person who I guess would do."

"You guess?" the Alligator Queen said, taking the telescope from her eye and bending over to leer at me. "In this court you have to say what you mean and mean it completely."

"Oh," I said. "Then I suppose—"

"Suppose?" the Alligator Queen said, her mouth one big curl exposing the brown shine of her teeth.

"That person is the one that I want," I said, shrugging. "Can you do it?"

The sound from the court wasn't the gentle snicker of leaves; there was uproar, vicious, angry, amused, and stinging. I bit my teeth into my lip and looked up at the Alligator Queen, who was now draped off her table, holding on only by the tips of her back claws, to look me in the eyes.

She seemed so familiar, so far up there. But I'd guessed I'd have known if I'd ever met an alligator before, and I'd thought I'd never had. Alligators, too, must fit somewhere in the pattern somehow, I thought, and that must mean everything does, and nothing at all is special. Not a single thing unless it's made so by someone else deciding so.

"Of course, I can do it," the Alligator Queen said, and the sound died down. "Of course, I can." She snapped back up to the top of her table to sit on her haunches, leaving only her tail to hang over the edge.

"Then we have a deal?" I asked.

"Bring her up," the Alligator Queen said. "And let me see what she's brought in return."

The band and the jesters slithered toward me, and before I could so much as pluck my own thumb or pull my own teeth from my lips, they had me in their claws and were boosting me up, first to the guard, then I was tossed to the ladies-in-waiting, swung up through the council, until at the very last, I was sitting across from the Alligator Queen on the vacant table.

HERE'S SOMETHING I REMEMBER from when I was young, very young. Probably the earliest memory I have. I know I am young because in it my mother comes home. Everyone gets attached to things when they're little like that. Children need to, to survive. Like little leeches. So, is it that extraordinary when a child loves its mother? When the mother is the whole world for the child? Or is it just the way it is because that's the way it is, and since that's the way it is, it's really not special at all? You don't choose your mother. Your mother doesn't choose you. Maybe later, maybe once the child can fend for itself, they can choose each other, and then maybe that means something. Something other than just the pattern of people repeating. Children just attach, and that's just how it is.

I was attached to a golden ball, when this memory occurs.

This rubber one, that squeaked out a sour burst of plastic-smelling air when I took it in my hand and squeezed.

My mother comes home in this memory and my father has placed the ball on a shelf so I can see it and not reach it. My arms are sore from reaching, I remember, and I don't look to my mother when she comes in, I am looking at this ball. I am trying to get it. I have been trying to get it for a long time, and I have been crying for a long time, and my father has been watching me do this, and at first I looked to him for help, but you know how fathers are, so he'd just sat on the couch, one leg propped on the other, and his chin held in his hand, watching. So, I stopped looking to him, and I don't look when my mother comes home, because I'm reaching for the ball.

"What are you doing?" my mother says in the memory when she sees me reaching and crying, but she's not talking to me, she's talking to my father. "Why don't you just give her the damn ball instead of sitting there and watching her cry?"

"She has to learn to cut it out," my father tells my mother. "She has to learn she can't have everything she wants."

But I don't learn to cut it out, as they are there, behind me, arguing, and things are crashing to the ground, and glass is shattering. I'm still reaching when the front door slams, and my father's office door slams, and the ball sits up on its shelf.

Whatever happened to that golden ball? I used to wonder from time to time. I'd never forgotten it, even though it'd been such a long time since I'd seen it.

I TOOK THE RING OUT of my pocket and held it out to the Alligator Queen, who poked the point of her nose at it and gave one mighty whiff.

"Where did this come from?" she asked, withdrawing back onto her own table.

"It was my mother's," I said.

"Then is it really yours to give?" asked the Alligator Queen.

Up on the top of the pyramid, sitting across from her, was like a different world made of just the two of us. Just her, sitting so tall that her head nearly brushed the burnt-out light fixture above, and I, on all fours, holding on to the edge of the table with one hand, the other holding the ring out over the space between the tables, afraid to move because the whole thing could topple down if I made any mistake.

"She left it a long time ago, and so it's mine now," I said.

"And you're fine with giving up something that was hers once to get what you want now?" the Alligator Queen asked. "Are you not concerned at all with how that would make her feel if she knew?"

"How can I know what she would feel if she knew?" I said. "She left me a long time ago, too, and now I hardly remember her. The feelings of someone you hardly remember are immaterial to the feelings you feel yourself."

"And how have you been feeling?" the Alligator Queen asked, and she took up her telescope again and fiddled with the lens.

"I have been wanting," I said.

"Well, I suppose that's part of your problem," the Alligator Queen said. "But you're not wanting your mother's ring?"

I shook my head and felt the table rock a little on its legs, so I stilled myself. It was very hard to still myself, especially when I was afraid. I couldn't understand how the Alligator Queen could sit there, flicking her tail, back and forth and back and forth, and have her table stay where it was. Why she didn't need to still herself.

"Give me the ring," the Alligator Queen said, and she leaned down and opened her mouth so it was level with my hand. Still I had to inch forward and reach as far as I could to slip it around one of her frontmost teeth.

She sat back up, rolling her jaw, running her tongue over her teeth, and getting used to the feel of the ring there. Then she lifted the telescope to her eye and pointed it in my direction. I watched myself in the lens, my face expanded and strange.

"There is something inside you that most people find hard to love," she confirmed for me.

She set the telescope back down across her lap and ran her tongue over the ring again. "I can help you get what you want, but you must do what I tell you, and we must remove the thing inside you."

"Go ahead and take it," I said.

"Not today," she said.

"Why not?" I asked.

"You should have to sit with something, for a little, before you decide to abandon it. You have to consider it, it and you, the feeling of it all," she said.

"I've never been sat with," I said. "You're making this up."

"So?" the Alligator Queen said. "We'll cut it out next week, at the dawn following the full moon. Come just after nightfall. Then come again the month after that. And the month after that. You must keep coming."

"How many times?" I asked.

"These things, they come back," the Alligator Queen said. "They always come back. If this is what you want, then you must keep coming back. You must keep removing, keep cutting."

"This is what I want," I said.

"Well, then, if you're so sure," the Alligator Queen said, and then she reached over, plucked me up, and handed me down to the council, who tossed me down to the ladies-in-waiting, who dropped me down to the guard, who dumped me into the many waiting claws of the jesters, as the band swung their instruments up and readied to play again. As I lay there, all I could see of the Alligator Queen was her tail, draped over the table and twitching.

"Then come back," she said from far away, and I was carried out of the court.

* * *

HERE IS THE START of it, what sends me to the court, or at least the start of what gets my coworker to tell me to go to the court:

We are closing together, he and I, and I am carrying a ream of unwrapped paper napkins between my hands, and as he is coming toward me and I'm going toward him, my hands either squeeze together too hard, or maybe they get too loose, I'm never sure, and the napkins break apart and go scattering everywhere, and he, laughing, kneels with me on the floor and helps me collect each one, and as we combine our messy stacks, his hands brush mine and I think *so*.

So, this is it.

So.

So, why not?

When he has gone back to work, I run the top-most napkin through my hands before wadding it into a ball and shoving it in my back pocket.

I SPENT THE NEXT week sitting with the thing inside me, trying to feel out what it was and what it would feel like to lose it, but mostly feeling nothing but that *so* in the back of my head, and fidgeting with my phone, and scrolling through messages, and telling the coworker who sent me to the court that it should be okay soon, that I had gone, that I had stood before them, and soon, I would have what I wanted, and so, that's all right, and she mostly didn't answer me back.

I was greeted at the doors of the mall by two guards, the moonlight skipping off the forks and knives around their necks. Inside I heard the band was in full swing, and all the fairy lights were flickering in time with the crash of the cymbals going ban-ban-ban, rest, ban-ban-ban. Toilet paper had been thrown about to drape off kiosks, and taped to hang here and there along the walls, and the lights shone through the paper, made it look like a rainbow, made it beautiful despite it being something so plain and disposable.

In the food court the pyramid had been disassembled and the

tables laid out in one long line near the boarded-up windows. All along the sides of the food court, the musicians wailed on their instruments, jaws waving and snapping, and the jesters bounced up and down, their stuffed-animal caps nodding to the beat, and on the floor the rest of the alligator court danced, and danced, and danced, spinning and lashing out tails and limbs, scales sparkling and leaving small trails of light like shooting stars as they whirled and moved.

When I approached, the Alligator Queen dropped to her belly, slithered her way through the dancers, and rose to her full height before me.

"Come," she said, taking me by the elbow.

"No one has ever liked it when I danced," I said. "Besides, I didn't come here to dance."

"You must indulge it, before the cutting. You must indulge me," she said, her long tail curling thrice around my hips before she spun me like a top into the crowd of alligators, and with the beat of the music in my ears, with the lights popping in my eyes, I simply forgot to stop spinning.

How long did I dance? I can't say. There are moments where everything is heat and pulse, and who can stop and count those moments? If you do, you kill them. That's not a rule that the Alligator Queen made. It's just how it is.

But when I came again into the Alligator Queen's claws, I was sweat covered and starving, and had somehow lost my shirt.

The alligators sat down at the tables with the Alligator Queen at the head. She motioned for me to sit on her righthand side, and so I did. In were brought platters the size of cribs under scuffed silver covertures, which were placed on the tables at even intervals. Even hidden like that, I could smell what it was. You could smell it all the way downtown and out in the suburbs both, I imagined. My skin was a hot towel smothering me from all the dancing. I pulled on my fingers, and my eyes roved over to the Alligator Queen, who looked to me, and then gave a nod to have the tops lifted off.

In heaps and piles, there were dead animals. Some whole, some half-whole, some just bits with bone sticking out, all draped in their own mangled guts. Cats, and birds, and little dogs, and in front of the Alligator Queen and me, a whole baby deer arranged neatly in the center of some smaller corpses, its chest split straight down the middle and cracked open to show its ribs and beyond.

"Go on," the Alligator Queen said. "Eat up."

I could've paused and said this isn't for me. This isn't what I'm supposed to eat. I could've hesitated. I could've tried to quiet the want and hunger.

But I did want, and I did hunger, so—

So, I stuck my hands into the deer's chest and wrapped my fingers around its heart and I pulled, and I—

And I dug in.

ONCE, AFTER MY MOTHER was gone, I got into my father's office. I was searching for something. The golden ball, maybe, I think, but who knows what is real and true past the fog that drifts in between your childhood and all that comes after. I tore it all apart, though, searching. Scattered his albums and clothes, his papers and books, his shot glasses and shotguns, his fine bottles of bourbon and his magazines of other women, spinning here and there, searching and reaching and grabbing and pulling, and he came home to find me among the tatters, lying on the floor with my chest heaving up and down, a little winded whirlwind, the exhausted cyclone, the uneasy eye of the storm.

And he didn't like that, no.

It must have been the golden ball. Perhaps he'd it hidden away. Perhaps my mother'd taken it when she left.

IN THE MORNING, THE Alligator Queen pulled me away from the court and into the massage parlor. There, there were no fairy lights, but the kind of lamps you find in dentist offices: too bright and built to swivel and search. First, she sat me down on the massage table and with a wet towel wiped the blood from my hands, my mouth, my neck, and my chest in gentle strokes. She gathered my hair up into a knot at the back of my head. She looked down her long jaw at me.

"Are you ready to cut it out?" she asked.

My stomach felt like an overblown beachball, and the air in the massage parlor was so cold against my damp chest. I wanted to curl up somewhere warm and safe and sleep. In a ball. In a bubble. *So,* I thought. *So, why not?*

"I suppose so," I said, my hands flapping on my thighs like wounded birds.

"Suppose," the Alligator Queen said. The ring around her tooth flashed in the bright light of the lamp she turned our way. "Who taught you to be so half-hearted?"

"Cut it out," I said. "It's what I came here for."

"You're the customer," she said. "You're the one who knows what you want, so you must be right."

She laid me down on my belly on the table, and I felt her claw resting right under my hairline where skull met neckbone.

"This will hurt," she said. "This will scar."

"But it will make me lovable?" I asked.

"More easy to love for some," she said. "But you'll have to wear a ribbon."

"Cut," I said, and her claw slit right under my skin and beyond, and the world popped and fizzled and burned, and I felt something coming out of me, something hard and cold like pebbles from the bottom of a riverbed, spilling to gather between my shoulders before overflowing down my spine.

When it was done, I lay there panting, listening to her clean up, the sound of whatever had come from me clacking and tinkling as she gathered them together and put them away. Then she pressed her snout to my neck and blew, and I felt the slit in my skin pucker like closing lips. She pulled me into a sitting position and brought me mirrors to look with.

An inch below my hairline, from just beneath the corner of one side of my jaw reaching all the way to the other, was a curved line, angry and bold. The Alligator Queen took out a floral-patterned ribbon and tied it around my neck to conceal it.

"Keep this on," she said. "And keep that secret."

SOMETIMES THERE WERE TIMES when yes, I would run screaming through the halls, and beat on our walls, beat and scream until the pictures fell, and my father would come, and you know how fathers are.

HERE ARE THINGS I didn't do, once I went to the Alligator Queen and she cut out of me what was hard to love:

I didn't fidget with the pens at work, and I didn't draw looping scribbles on the back of crumpled-up receipts, and I didn't bother my coworker with talk about anything other than the weather, and I didn't pace, and I didn't look people directly in the eye too long when they smiled at me, or stare just above their heads or at the floor if they didn't smile at me, and I didn't pull at my fingers, and I didn't bite my lips, and I didn't flinch, or flutter my hands in front of my face when I spoke, and I didn't feel a need to pick everything up, and fondle it, and maybe put it in my purse, or down my bra, or in my shoe, or anywhere else, and I didn't feel the need to follow anyone on the street, and I didn't feel the need to look up at the sun, and I didn't feel a need to look up at the moon, and I didn't look away right away when he looked my way, and neither did I look too long his way when he looked my way, and I didn't look his way too often at all, but I stood very still, and I breathed a lot, deep quiet breaths, and I pressed my lips together and touched my fingertips to the bow around my neck, and I nodded when people spoke to me, and I went *mmmhm*, or *I guess so* when he asked me things, and I sat very still. I sat very still next to him on break and I sat very still next to him in the car and I sat very still across from him at dinner and then I lay very still next to him in bed and after, he lay there laughing, and told me that the way I used to look at him was so frightening sometimes, that I had been so frightening sometimes, like there was another thing behind my eyes that had been so hungry, and he trailed his fingers over the bow around my neck, and I took his hand from there, and I laid it on my breast, and I breathed, and I slept.

JUST BEFORE THE FULL moon my hands started to fly again. They started to inch ever so little away from my body and out back into the world, and then my eyes, they began to rove, and I looked at paper, and it looked blindingly bare, and I looked at the people, and they looked hatefully similar, and I looked in the mirror and saw my eyes as something frightening, and I knew it was time to go back to the mall.

YOU UNDERSTAND HOW IT can be when you're small, and how fathers can be when you are small, and it is just the two of you, and he will not look at you too often, as if there is something in you that is hard to look at, as if you are someone else who was once hard to look at, and how he will only look if you are fidgeting, or reaching, or getting into something you ought not get into, and how finally, when you have gotten in too far, he will come and he will touch, but it will only be to pick you up and put you in a room and close that room up.

IN NOVEMBER, WE WENT to the old clothing store, the Alligator Queen, the court, and I, and we ran from one another between the stacks of jeans and shirts, the displays of watches and ties, because sometimes these things have to be indulged, the Alligator Queen said. We dodged around the carousels of dresses, and sometimes hid underneath them to burst out and surprise each other, jaws snapping, hissing between our teeth, and in our springs and our shocks, we'd knock the dresses over, where we'd leave them to lie as we chased and were chased again.

And then came the feast, where, hot and panting, I ate until I was sated, and ate, and then ate again.

And then came the cutting, where for the first time since the moon rose, I thought of him. And I asked the Alligator Queen why it was that only women came to the court, and she, touching her claw to the back of my neck, said maybe there was something in women that understood alligators, and something in alligators that understood women.

"After all, when we get too big, when we get too frightening, or when people get too tired of us, we both get flushed down the shitter," she said, and laughed, my mother's ring bouncing on her tooth.

"Why are you all women? Where are your men? Aren't you worried about dying out?"

"Why worry about that, when there's plenty else to be feeling in the here and now?" the Alligator Queen said. "You worry too much. Quiet. Now it's time to cut it out."

She laid me down, and I felt her slit the scar open across the back of my neck, and I felt it all spilling out again until I was empty.

IN DECEMBER, HE GAVE me a package of black socks for work because he said he saw mine had been wearing out and I held the package steady in my hands, and said thank you, I love them, and I gave him new fuses in return, and then, with his hand on the back of my neck just below the ribbon, we went together upstairs and shut off all the lights.

WHEN MY FATHER CAME home alone that first time, I think I had watched from the window, and I had run at him, I had run past him, I had beat upon the door, I had reached up toward the gold-plated knob, and I had been crying, yes, I had been crying and reaching for a long time, and he took me by the elbow and pulled me back, telling me to cut it out, goddammit, cut it out.

IN FEBRUARY WE, THE Alligator Queen, the court, and I, made ourselves a swamp by jamming up the cracks under the bathroom door and clogging all the toilets, and we floated there, me in an innertube by the Alligator Queen, and her on her back, showing me her belly, and she reached her tail up and brushed it down my leg and said that I'm so soft, much too soft, and I put a hand on her belly and said there were soft parts to her, too, and she said, "Ah, yes, but I can conceal those if I want to," and rolled over with a wink before sinking below the toilet water.

IN APRIL, HE SIGHED and watched me sit across the room and asked me is this all there is?

He told me there was something more to me, once, he thought.

He wondered aloud where it went, and I twirled the end of my ribbon around my finger and sat watching the pictures on the TV.

PARENTS DON'T CHOOSE THEIR children, and children don't choose their parents, and there is nothing special there, nothing special at all, so I should not hate my mother for leaving me, and should not want to be chosen, you understand, except that everyone wants to be chosen, everyone wants to be seen and be loved, and that isn't so strange, is it? You understand?

THE ALLIGATOR QUEEN SPAT a chewed-up chicken head out of her mouth in May and looked at me, and asked was I really sure that it'd been my mother's choice to leave at all?

IN JUNE, I SAT in the bathroom, running my thumb along the ribbon and staring at the plastic stick in my hand that I'd just pissed on. The results took shape at such a speed that had it been the day before the full moon, surely I would have been tugging my fingers and biting my lip and fretting, fretting, fretting, but it was not the day before the full moon, so I sat there quietly, and I watched the lines come into view, before going out to tell him.

YOU KNOW HOW FATHERS are.

IN JUNE, DID THE Alligator Queen eye my stomach? Did she grimace as she sat me down on the massage table? Did she know?

She did touch her claws to my skull and massage my scalp with their tips. She did tell me this:

"Everyone has more than one brain, you know. They have a reptile brain wrapped up in all that primate slush. A thinking and watching and moving and striving to live brain. A vicious and wanting and taking brain. A brain that sees patterns. A brain that sees dangers. A brain that has longing as thick and old as mud, as natural and hot as blood, as all-consuming as they are ever-hungry. Everyone has it and some have more of it than others, and who can say why, though doctors in their white coats will hazard their guesses and have their say-sos, and people will make their judgments. There will always be say-sos and judgments.

"Are you sure this is what you want?" she asked.

"It's what I came here for," I said.

"But you don't have to leave here with it," she said.

"Cut it out," I said.

She laid me on the table, and she did so, and when it all click-clacked out of me, and she swept it all away, I sat up, and she put something in my palm.

"I saw this and thought of you," she said. "I thought you'd want it."

In my palm was a ball, rubber and golden. I squeezed it once and it squeaked pathetically. I put it in my bag and told her thank you, I loved it, then I tied back on my ribbon.

But of course, I didn't want it then. Of course, I didn't.

IN JULY HE THREW his hands up and asked how could he have a child with me when he felt like he didn't even know me, how could he be expected to make that kind of commitment, and I sat and caressed the ribbon, and watched him as he paced, and he pulled at his hair, and as he knelt down in front of me, and asked where was I? In all of this? Said it was as if there was nothing behind my eyes.

And I asked him,

"Do you really want to see me?"

And put his hand to my bow.

And he said, "Sure, I love you, I do."

"Wait," I told him, and I guided his hand in undoing my ribbon.

IN AUGUST, I DIDN'T go to the court.

MAYBE WOMEN UNDERSTAND SOMETHING about alligators and maybe alligators understand something about women, and maybe we are both just rolling over and sinking into the swamp, maybe we are both just turning soft and turning hard and spinning, and spinning, and thrashing, and wanting.

IN SEPTEMBER, MY HANDS tumbled out in front of me in one great rolling wave as I pleaded, and as I cried, and as I yelled, and as I paced, and the swelling in my stomach felt fit to burst, and yet I hungered still, and yet I wanted still, and there was never enough. My fingers snapped closed on empty air, my teeth tore into nothing, and he sat on the couch, watching me, and I could see that look in his eye, that look that I had thought meant something other than *you're so frightening sometimes*, that I thought had meant he had seen me, as one single thing in the pattern of things, and he had been looking closer.

"Cut it out," I yelled, "cut it out, goddammit, cut it out!"

After he made his way out the door and shut it with a bang that rocked the walls, I thrashed and kicked and spun and tore, and eventually my foot caught my purse, and my purse went flying, and when it landed, out rolled the golden ball.

I didn't see it until I had tired myself out and I was lying there, among the wreck of what I had done. By then I was far too worn out, and it was far too far away for me to do anything other than reach my hand out in its direction.

MAYBE ALLIGATORS AND WOMEN have an understanding, maybe alligators and women are far closer in the repeating pattern of it all than we tend to think, maybe alligators and women—we both get flushed down the shitter in the end.

You understand?

YOU KNOW HOW FATHERS are.

WHEN I NEXT CAME to the mall with the golden ball and the tattered ribbon in my hand there was no music beyond the doors, and the fairy lights were all eaten up by the bright noon hour, which strong-armed its way through the cracks between the boards on the windows and doors. Still, I made my way to the court of the Alligator Queen, carrying what spoils she had given me in one hand, and the hump of my stomach in the other.

When I got to the court, there were no alligators on the pyramid of tables, or dancing on pointed claws across the tiles, or slithering through the halls and stores, or floating in their bathroom swamp.

Instead, standing on the food court floor, there were women. Naked, their bodies rolling soft mounds of flesh and sweat, turning this way and that, and swaying on spot as they gathered up their hair in their hands and let it fall, or as they stretched their arms and cracked their fingers, reaching their palms toward the slanted light streaming through the boards with hunger.

At their feet there were skins covered in scales, as many skins as there were bodies of women, as many skins as there had been alligators in the alligator court. Save for one, I saw.

And then came from behind me, a voice familiar but unique, known but unrecognized, and it said,

"Turn around, child, and let yourself look at me."

And so, I did. And there was the Alligator Queen, standing on her back legs and looking down her pointed nose at me. She took the claw she used for cutting, put it to her own soft underside, and slit herself from the tip of her collarbone down to the top of her tail. She opened up and then she stepped out of herself, letting her scales clatter to the ground.

"Do you see me?" she asked. "Do you know me?"

And of course, I did, of course.

IT IS THE CHOOSING that matters, you know, the seeing the pattern, and seeing someone in the pattern, and then choosing that person out of that whole pattern, and seeing them separate and whole, and not looking away.

* * *

SHE BROUGHT ME INTO the massage parlor once more, my hand in her hand, and once we were inside, she touched my stomach and I touched her face and we did cry, yes, for a little, and she told me I was soft, much too soft, and I touched her wet cheek and told her she was soft, too. But she could, she reminded me, hide it. There were ways. There were systems in place, she told me. And then she brought out a silver bowl, and set it on the massage table, and she said,

"I saved these for you."

In the bowl there were scales of all the deepest shades of green, laced with iridescent sparks of bruised blue when they caught the light right, and deep tumors of black when they sat in shadow. Atop them all sat my mother's ring.

I put my hand atop the scales, brushed the ring with my fingertips.

"What do you want in return?" I asked. "The golden ball? The ribbon?"

"Those were gifts I gave to you," she said. "Gifts cannot be given back."

"The ring," I said.

"Was never wholly yours to give," she said. "And so, I am already owed." She touched my stomach, and she put a hand atop my head, and looked me in the eyes. "There is a seat next to me waiting vacant, and I am owed two things now, if this is what you want."

I set aside the ribbon and the golden ball. I took up the ring in one hand, and a scale in the other. Felt their weight and permeance. I held them up to the light and saw how beautiful they were to see.

But what of the fetus? What of the child? Would she be scaled? Or would she be soft and flesh? And what would any of that mean for her? And what if she didn't come out a her at all? We all know fathers, know where they come from, and know there are none in the Alligator Queen's court.

The Alligator Queen stood before me, one hand resting where the fetus waited in my belly, the other hand resting on the crown of my head, beneath which my brains were doing their ticking. She had her eyes open and on me and an open offer waiting on the table. There was a choice there to be made. And it would set me down one path or another with no way to know what lay at either's end.

"Is this what you want?" the Alligator Queen asked me. "Do we have a deal?"

Mothers don't choose their children. Children don't choose their mothers. They're all just part of that pattern, you know, repeating, mother to child mother to child. They don't choose each other, unless they actually do.

And so, I chose.

And it's a choice you could make, too, you know. Do you understand?

The Nature of Her Identity

Jude Rittenhouse

I.
No matter what she believed,
she remembered being a cypress:

roots tangled like fists around stones.
Growth mangled and guided

by a deceased glacier's scree field.
The slender shoot of her

growing trunk pushing, insistent,
belligerent. She even recalled splitting

a crack in blackness: her body broke
a boulder; light's patient tongues

stroked bruised shoulders. Maybe you
believe in past lives; maybe not.

Facts can't prove anything complex.
We're all made of guesses. She knew

whales, elephants, goats, maples
were her first cousins. Knew

we're all born to sing low or high
notes through air's blue throat. She

felt lungs and pulse respond to rain,
waves, babies of every species:

wet preparation. Even spiders
join this choir as they squeeze out

threads: fresh-woven homes,
traps, temporary thrones. She forgot

what ended her existence
as a tree: wind, lightning, time

to learn another way of being braided
into life. Singular. Wild. She didn't

recall which initiation, incarnation or
losses taught her kindness. Maybe,

like her being a cypress, we're all still
busting through granite to find that light.

II.
She emerged from tenebrous forests
to start a new page made of green.

Not the color. The vibration
jade emanates after that brass bowl

of being stops ringing. What you think
matters. She felt thoughts

people didn't know they believed. Strange
gifts fall to each of us like ripe peaches;

fuzz and bruises often intervene between
desire and sweet juices. Otherwise life

would be a riff without chorus or instruments.
Silence is the sound of tenderness: the softest

aqua of sky and sea far from any solid place
where they might meet. What we expect

is exactly what we will or won't see
no matter what hue our lover breathes this

unforeseen morning. She listened with her skin
to discover a new beginning. Meaning

is what we find and seek when we cease
hearing eternity in wave after wave after wave.

She heeded earth's primordial whisper: *Fill
the void; become kind and brave.*

III.
Maples waved. Cumulus colonies shape-shifted.
Wind made time's true nature visible. A girl believed

them. Sky's remoteness a safer home, she flew there.
Stayed hours, days. Left behind all that bruised-blue

noise, each deaf and absent presence. Kept watching
until she stopped

looking for what she was already
more than. Stopped believing garbled myths, returned

to earth and *saw* humanity's clamor: armor. A glinting,
clanging distraction. A terrible trembling

rusted inside by unshed tears. Having seen the shapes
behind sound, words seemed nothing but a pack of pesky

saints. Made up. We each respond to icons in predictably
unpredictable ways. You can think

anything. She was a priestess, a witch. Her incantations
helped trees breathe. Helped men feel disavowed

fevers. Made a field where humans could become
a sunrise chorale, ocean's clergy, wind's favorite memory.

A Selkie's Tale

Hannah Yang

IN HIS WORLD, EVERYONE WEARS SO MANY DIFFERENT SKINS. AFTER ALL these years I still can't get used to it.

Cotton skins. Polyester skins. Rubber skins in stormy weather. Painted skins of creams and powders to hide every blemish. Bare skin after a shower, soft to the touch, with those thin blue veins underneath.

EVERY MOM AT FIA'S play group wears a variation on the same theme. Black leggings, Nike sneakers, and a puffy winter jacket. Sometimes Starbucks in one hand. Our mom outfits, we call them.

Today when I go to pick up Fia, there's a new mom standing in the lounge. She wears a long patchwork dress that flows down to her ankles. She doesn't join us in the front lounge as we chat about our kids, our vacation plans, new restaurants in town we've been meaning to try. Instead she just stands there, staring at her son through the window, the new redheaded boy playing in the corner.

She's like me. I look at her and I know. It's not the weird outfit, it's something deeper, recognizable, that silent song of a person who belongs to a faraway home and can't go back. There's something of hers being held for ransom.

I'm not proud of it, but I hide. Position myself behind the other moms so I'm not in her line of sight.

When the doors open, Fia hurtles toward me, all open arms and pink cheeks, clutching Pet in one hand, a stuffed animal that used to be white once but is now the color of dryer lint. I scoop her up and make my getaway, but not fast enough. The new woman follows us out the door and into the parking lot, jogging to keep up with us. Her son hasn't even come outside yet.

"Hi," she says.

I pretend not to hear her.

"Hi," she repeats, more loudly this time.

"Oh, hey. Sorry, I can't really chat, we're in a bit of a rush."

"Of course. I totally understand. It's just that we just moved here and don't really know anyone yet. Are you new here too? How old's your little one?"

I unlock the car, strap Fia into her car seat. I fight back the urge to shield Fia's eyes, the same way I would if there were something inappropriate on TV. "Look, I'm afraid I've really got to run."

The woman takes a step back and smiles, a plastic-wrapped smile. She might not have the mom outfit, but she has the mom smile down pat.

For a moment I wonder if I'm crazy to think she's anything like me. If I'm simply projecting my own thoughts onto her face. Maybe I've reached the point where everywhere I go, I see mirrors.

Then she grabs my arm so hard that it hurts. Pulls me in closer, and I know I was right after all.

"Help me," she whispers.

"I don't know what you mean."

"You're one of us, aren't you?"

I pull my arm free. "Stop it. You're hurting me."

She lets go. I expect her to be angry, but instead she only looks bewildered.

I slide into my seat and slam the door shut. It takes me three tries to get the key into the ignition. My hands are shaking. The woman stands in the parking lot and watches us pull away.

Fia frowns at me in the rearview mirror. "Who was that lady, Mama?"

"Don't listen to her, baby. Some people are just crazy."

But all the long drive home, I hear her words replaying in my head. And I know I won't be able to avoid her forever.

Somewhere in this town, there lives another woman like me.

SEAN STAYS LATE IN the office again. He doesn't come home until after I've given Fia her bath, put her to bed, and cleared all the dishes. The house only shows Sean its good side. He rarely sees it naked, cereal spilled across the granite counters, toys uncleared on the living room floor.

At night I watch him sleep. Belly-up, mouth open.

I didn't notice when he stole my skin. My mother would have called me foolish for that, if she ever found out that I went so long without noticing. Too foolish to be a true daughter of hers. Too simple-minded, easily tricked.

She'd be right, I suppose. My only excuse is that for him, I stepped in and out of my skin so many times that I stopped paying attention. It began to feel normal when he asked me to go without it for a few hours at a time, then a few days, then a full week.

The first time, it was for only a moment, just long enough to feel his touch underneath. He didn't ask me to do it. That was why I decided to, though I'd said no to all the other men before him, the ones who had begged and pleaded to see me bare. We stood on the border between what was his and what was mine, and in that in-between place I peeled off my skin. Stepped out onto the sunbaked sand. Let him put his calloused hand on top of my own.

Our first touch was so gentle that the sensation was almost more like a sound, the barest crinkling, no louder than the brush of a bird's wing against an updraft.

How could I notice anything else, beyond the spider-silk longing of that sound?

* * *

THE NEW MOM'S NAME is Colleen. I find this out from the play group director. I only asked about her because I like to be able to put a name to my fears. It feels less threatening, somehow, more human. I don't know when more human started to mean less threatening. It's like my sense of direction has turned backwards.

For two weeks, we dance around each other, almost as if someone's choreographed it. We drop off our children at eight, pick them up again at four, and never speak a word to one another. Sometimes I catch her looking at me out of the corner of her eye when I go to pick up Fia. It's not the staring I notice, but the evasion, how every time I raise my head she looks away.

I can't stop thinking about her. Somewhere inside me there's a bright, reckless feeling, that feeling of looking at a stove burner and wanting to touch. Of standing on a balcony and wanting to jump.

At last, I bend. I stand next to her during drop-off. We watch our kids play through the glass.

"Listen," she says. "I didn't mean to scare you last time."

"We can't talk now," I say. "Not where they'll hear. Let me take you out for coffee."

I take her to the Starbucks in my own neighborhood. We sit on the stools in front of the window, through which we see an endless row of white picket fences and neatly trimmed lawns. It is painfully clear, here, how structured and domestic both of our lives have become. How far we are from the sea.

I take a sip. The coffee is too hot, singes the taste buds right off my tongue.

Colleen's only a few years younger than I am, but the slim difference seems stark now. She has such wide eyes, such a naive face. Like she still thinks there's something better than this in store for her.

She breaks the ice bluntly. "I can't do this anymore. I thought it would get easier, but it doesn't ever let up."

"I wasn't meant for motherhood either. Nobody is. Most days, maternal instinct is just a lie women tell each other so we don't go mad. You grow into it slowly."

"We could escape together," she says. "Force our husbands to tell us where our skins are. Leave this place behind and go home."

"Our kids need us. Think about Billy. It's not his fault, what his father did to you."

Her Billy is a solemn little boy, with big ears and a bright shock of ginger hair, always playing by himself. He's three and a half years old, the same as Fia. Is three and a half old enough to understand your mother abandoning you? Is three and a half even old enough to remember her afterward?

Her hands tremble around the mug. "I love Billy. But I need to love myself too. Doesn't that mean anything?"

"Just hold out a little longer," I say, softening my voice. "It got better for me. I'm sure it will get better for you, too."

"Of course," she says. "Of course you're right."

Two women, both lying through our teeth.

AFTERWARD, I THROW MYSELF into the art of loving my home. I chose all the décor on my own. Wallpaper the perfect shade of cream. Drapes trimmed with golden fringe. A patent-leather loveseat the perfect size for two.

I sweep the floor. Dust the shelves. Wipe the countertops until they sparkle. There is poetry in cleanliness. But if I am an artist, I am an artist fighting against time, because the whole house seeks to destroy my creation. It turns its teeth inward and eats away at itself.

Keeping Fia alive and healthy is the same kind of struggle. She's always swallowing things she shouldn't, climbing onto things she shouldn't, putting everything she can find up her nose. It's a relief to get her out of her bath and tuck her into bed, like clicking Save on an important document and putting it away for the night.

Sean comes home late again, but this time I stay up waiting for him. When I hear the door open, I take the shepherd's pie out of the oven and set it on the table.

"Did you have a good day?" he says. He's in a good mood.

"Sure."

"Where'd you go?" he says. His voice casual, only slightly possessive.

"What do you mean?"

"I tried calling home this morning and nobody picked up."

"Oh, I just went out with some new friends. Other moms." It's not quite a lie, and there is safety in this plurality.

He gives me a suspicious look. He knows I don't have friends, at least not ones I do more than pay lip service to. He knows that until now, my days were always the same. For a moment, I worry that he might question me more.

But he keeps his voice mild. "You should invite them over sometime. We haven't hosted anybody in a while."

He eats his shepherd's pie in a few bites, ravenous in a way I'll never understand. Sean is always hungry, always wants more. He leaves only crumbs behind. Drains his beer in a single swig and then slides the glass down next to his plate.

We've settled into a routine, me and Sean and Fia, three lives intertwined. To untangle us now would be like erasing an old work of art. Not a masterpiece, not even particularly beautiful, but old enough to have survived this long. It would take an act of deliberate cruelty to destroy something like this.

More dishes to be washed. More groceries to be bought. It's a pattern I find comforting, like the tide coming in and out. Round and round and round we go.

COLLEEN AND I MEET for coffee nearly every morning now, while the kids are at play group. Sometimes we go in the afternoon, if we have something else to do in the mornings. We choose moments when our husbands won't notice, stolen hours.

We speak of how fast our kids are growing, of the milestones we hope to see them hit someday, graduations and weddings and promotions. Sometimes we talk for so long that I call our babysitter and ask her to pick Fia up from her play group.

The one thing we never speak of is home. That topic is off-limits to us, too raw and too painful to touch.

There's something illicit about it anyway, even the most mundane of our conversations. Some kind of magic created by the meeting of two women from a world different from this one. It brings out a part of me that I had thought to be dead.

This time, we migrate from Starbucks to the bar a few blocks away. It's a casual spot, with exposed lighting and graffitied woodwork. Most of the customers are gaggles of undergraduates pre-gaming for something else, doing rounds of shots.

We pick a booth in the back corner, tucked away, and order one bottle of red wine, then another. My tolerance is shot; I haven't had alcohol since having Fia, except for champagne on New Year's. After a while the wine grips me by the throat, forces me into some form of honesty.

"I know where my real skin is," I confess to her.

She drops her voice. "When did you find it?"

"Oh, years ago. You think Sean can hide anything from me? We've been married so long it's like there are hardly any secrets between us."

"If you've known all this time, why haven't you gone home yet?"

"There's no reason to. I love my life here. Besides, I would never leave Fia behind."

She looks away. "Billy will be better off without me. His father loves him. And he'll understand someday, won't he?"

"You can't think that way. That's like giving up."

She takes another sip, wipes her mouth. "I've searched for mine. Every time he goes to work. I still haven't found it."

"They don't always keep it in the house, you know. Maybe he asked one of his friends to hold onto it for him. Or his parents. Have you tried looking at their place?"

"You think my husband would ever allow that? Whenever we're with his family, he hardly lets me out of his sight."

I reach out across the table, hold her hand. Our fingers intertwine. Human fingers with calloused tips, perfect for holding wineglasses and changing diapers and cutting fruit into bite-sized pieces for three-year-old mouths. A symbol of what we've gained. A reminder of what we've lost.

I don't notice the time until the undergraduates start tripping over themselves on the way to the bathroom. By the time I check my phone, it's ten thirty, long past when Sean would be home. Seven missed calls, the notification ominous and glaring on my screen.

"Shit," I say. "I have to go."

"Call me later?" she says, but I'm already out the door.

SEAN IS PACING BY the time I get home, never a good sign. The viscera of Chinese takeout are scattered across the kitchen table.

He says, deathly quiet, "Where have you been?"

"Where's Fia?"

"Already in bed, of course. I sent the babysitter home. And don't think I didn't notice that you didn't answer my question."

"I was just out with friends. We lost track of time," I say.

"So you can just neglect your duties at home?"

"What, am I not allowed to have friends now?"

"You've been seeing a lot of these friends lately. Are you sure they're just friends?"

"What's that supposed to mean?" I take a step back.

He steps forward at the same time, so that his face is only inches away from mine. He sniffs, and his brow darkens. "Have you been drinking?"

The tension is broken by a noise from the staircase. Fia stands there, bleary-eyed in her pink pajamas, clutching Pet. "Daddy?"

I move toward her, but Sean beats me there. His mood softens all at once, the way it always does when he's with Fia. He picks her up and brushes her hair out of her face. "Did we wake you up?"

"You were being too loud," she says, an accusation.

"Don't worry about that, nugget. What have you and Pet been up to?"

"I had a good sleep. But Pet had a bad dream."

"Oh no. Let's see if we can fix that, shall we?"

He swings Fia around in a wide arc until she's laughing again. She hardly ever sees him now, he's so busy at work, but that's only made her love grow more, not less. She dotes on her father, clings to every moment of him that he gives her. Sometimes I worry that Fia will turn out a little too much like me.

While he cheers her up, I put away his takeout boxes. There's a whole stack of dirty dishes I haven't had time to wash in the past couple of days, but I don't have the energy to deal with them right now. I chose this life, I remind myself. I still choose this.

THE TRUTH IS THAT I didn't find my skin on my own. Sean told me where it was, the day before we were married. He was different then, just a boy, suntanned from days on the beach, eyes bright and earnest.

"It will always be there if you want it," he said. "You can take it and go home."

"How do you know I won't?"

He was quiet for a moment. "I guess I don't. But I know I want this to be real. I want to know that you're staying because you want to, not because you have no other options."

I thought that was romantic. I remember wondering how, out of all mankind, I had fallen for the only person who would trust a creature like me enough to let me step into his life without my hands tied.

In the heat of that romance, I'd almost forgotten about the theft itself. The fact that Sean stole my skin before he gave it back. The hurt of it when I realized what he'd done, bright and desperate, like realizing you've been left adrift in the ocean with no land in sight.

After we put Fia to bed he seems sorry for yelling, though he doesn't say it. Sex tonight is slow and gentle, like we're kids again, exploring one another for the first time. It takes me back to that first summer on the beach, before there was anything between us that had to be taken or given. When Sean was just a boy who believed in magic and in marriage and truly thought the two could coexist.

He falls asleep still naked, all our limbs intertwined. Sometimes, in the busyness of our lives now, I forget this side of him, this tenderness. Forget the more subtle ways in which he has the power to make me stay. The way he looks at me as if I am the only one here. The gentle way he treats our child. And I know what I have to do.

AFTER SEAN IS ASLEEP, I call her. She picks up on the first ring.

I haven't yet decided what to say. She doesn't speak either. Nothing but our quiet breathing across the line, not quite in sync, in and out, in and out.

IN THE MIDDLE OF the night, I open the front door. It feels like sticking my head into the freezer, a bone-shiver chill. I wrap my jacket tighter around myself as I step out into the porch.

The clouds have obscured the stars, so the only hint of light comes from the porch lights left on by our neighbors. A darkness like watered-down ink, thin and nascent. Everything is still.

At first I think she's decided not to come, but then I see her, a lone figure standing straight-backed in the dark. She's brought a small backpack with her, nothing more.

She steps toward me. I give her my true skin.

Softly, quickly, runs her fingers over what once was mine. When she finally speaks, her voice is a hoarse whisper. "You won't need this someday?"

I shake my head, a gesture that I realize too late could be interpreted as both a yes and a no, but she seems to take it in stride.

"What if you wake up one day and realize you miss home?"

"I am home."

It's true. I am. But a piece of me will follow her, too.

I watch her walk away. She turns around and waves, once. Then she rounds the bend, and I can't see her anymore.

I picture her stepping onto the surf. Picture her wrapping my skin around herself and letting it seal around her body, until once again she is whole. By morning, perhaps, she will have reached the place where the sky meets the sea.

I join Sean in bed, but I can't fall asleep. The clock in the living room ticks quietly. Sean snores beside me, rolls over, keeps snoring. Fia sleeps in her small canopy bed, one hand curled around Pet. The house is calm and still and mine.

I go to the kitchen and wash the dishes from the past couple of days. There's a crust on the side of one pan that won't come off, no matter how hard I scrub. The hot water leaves my hands raw and wrinkled. I pick at the callus on the pad of my finger. A sliver of skin comes off, thin and white, exposing the red raw burning underneath. Skin under skin under skin.

pretty

Sophia Slattery

don't call her pretty.

a shallow attempt
to liken her
essence
energy
aura
to a meaningless word,
derived from solely the physical

tell her,

her presence is infectious,
radiant
to be around her is to bask in her precious pheromones
enlightening all in her company
she carries surrounding her a tangible light
which she shares altruistically

that when she is passionate,
her fierceness could make mountains quiver
her power is that,
that if she reached for the stars
you know undoubtedly, she could grasp them as,
after all
her soul is comprised of them

that when she is sad,
as inevitably at some point she will be,
your heart yearns to provide any semblance of comfort
and you wonder,
how anyone or anything could ever desire
to dampen the incredible light
of her luminous being

that when she loves something,
it should consider itself
extraordinarily lucky
because her heart is endless in its capacity to love,
and surround others with tenderness
and to simply know her
be around her
and feel the capability of that heart
is to love her

don't call her pretty.

Ann, Without

Broderick Eaton

ANN WITHOUT AN *E* GLARES ACROSS THE CAFÉ AT ANNE WITH AN *E*. ANN without an *e* has always wished her name had an *e*. Anne with an *e* has an *e*. Anne with an *e* has it all.

Ann, without an *e* to echo the extra-ness of having an *e* with the same fanfare of townes and shoppes that are always olde and sound like fancy places to drink frappes and talk about jewels and extravagant vacations, stares hard at the chip in the lip of her brown mug. Anne with an *e* probably doesn't have a chip in her mug like this one that keeps funneling drops of coffee to land on Ann without an *e*'s lap before a good swallow has a chance to roll across her tongue. The coffee's bitter warmth is lost on the barren wasteland of her third-best pants with the purple thread running down the outside seam that she sewed in from the knee to the ankle, in an effort to get Thomas to look at her again, to get him to notice the results of all those new Zumba classes at the Y that she's been going to since he started working longer and longer hours and sometimes had one excuse or another to not come home at all.

The image of herself seated at the old Singer, bent over the pulled-apart denim and tough purple thread, working like her entire Home-Ec grade depended on the straightness of her lines and the closeness of her loops to hold the parts together, seems a little desperate now.

Well, she failed that project anyway. It was never about the pants. The seams came undone, but not of the pants, which she now wears with the same determined flash of color as any warpaint in history smeared from finger to cheek, but of the marriage they had stood on either side of and passively stared at for more years than either of them wanted to admit. They would have to acknowledge that they'd both let it deteriorate like a car left parked and unmoved until its tires begin to slacken, though no one notices until the frame suddenly reclines to one side more than the other and the terminal stain is discovered seeping into the pavement below.

Thomas now sits across from Anne with an *e*, his back to his wife without an *e* several tables away. Anne With looks up and makes brief eye contact with Ann Without. No sign of recognition or discomfort crosses her pretty face, so Thomas probably hasn't mentioned that he's married. That he's been married for fourteen years. Anne with an *e* doesn't know she's looking at her namesake who is one letter short of having everything.

Anne With lets her eyes drop back to the conversation she's having with Ann Without's husband, though her gaze nervously flits back up a couple of times to see if Ann Without is still looking at her.

She is.

Ann Without watches them order. Anne With crinkles the corners of her eyes at the waitress and Thomas shifts against the back of his chair in a way that allows him to slump a little as his groin pushes toward Anne With under the little round table as the waitress walks away smiling. Their legs touch and Anne's hand traces circles on his knee. It's a casual, familiar move.

What does she see in him? Ann Without can hardly fault her, though, because she herself was drawn to his borderline helplessness, his almost humanness, that made him appealing in the way that a sullen dog at the pound sits in the corner, unafraid but certainly not effusive, and somehow gets adopted by someone bent on rescuing a creature that might not actually feel itself in need of rescuing in the first place. From the moment Ann Without met Thomas, she saw him as a scribbled sort of person who didn't really know what he wanted ahead of time but definitely knew what he didn't want after the fact. The kind of man who passively bobs along the surface like a jellyfish without making any real decisions for himself, but who is also quick to point out when things aren't to his liking.

When she planned their honeymoon after giving up on getting his input, she was giddy to tell him about the cabin in the mountains that she'd reserved. A few days of being alone, just the two of them, sounded like a fine way to start their marriage.

"It sounds cold," was all he had to say.

She rebooked a cottage at the beach.

"It's always cloudy."

She scheduled four nights at a casino resort where they could eat buffet dinners and watch recognized singers wrap up their dwindling careers by performing for small audiences as cocktails and smoke made the rounds of the room. She chose not to tell him where they were going until they were on the road and he realized he didn't know the plan and it was easier for him to just go along with what Ann without an *e* had planned for them both.

Little did she know, this was just the preamble to a long lack of planning together, a day to day of Ann speaking for both of them and looking for his satisfaction in the results of her efforts. She made plans, he complained about the details, and they ended up doing things and usually having a decent time. It was okay, she told herself, it wasn't like they fought or worried about outcomes. By dropping her unrealistic vision of great, she found she could live with good enough.

And now he's ditching her without so much as the courtesy of a conversation. She saw the text on his phone this morning that confirmed what she'd already begun to assume. *Hi Love, Rosie's for lunch, 12:30?* But she didn't know the other woman had her name, only with that *e* that changes everything. And Anne not only has an *e*, but Ann's husband now, too.

Ann Without is startled back to herself by the appearance of the waitress's coffee pot under her nose to refill the chipped mug. She considers asking for a new mug that maybe doesn't have a spot in it that causes her pants to bear the discoloration of coffee, but she doesn't want to be a bother. She can just turn the mug around and drink from the other side.

The way she jumps in surprise makes her chair squeak against the floor and several people look up, including Anne, whose *e* practically hovers over her head like a halo. Even Thomas half turns her direction, enough that she is reminded how much face he has on so little territory of his head, leaving a remarkable amount of head without face. It's a little odd, distracting even, but she'd not really paid attention to the extent of it before. It was part and parcel of the whole Thomas. Now his small face feels like settling for so much less than great that she wonders how she ever convinced herself they were good together at all. Maybe she deserves someone whose face is stretched into more normal proportions and whose eyes would meet hers as they spoke to one another.

Ann Without notes with cheerless, but nonetheless gratifying, satisfaction that he's not really looking at Anne With as they chat, either.

She wonders what Thomas might have noticed about herself that he just put up with. What did he settle for as their marriage crawled through the first decade and into the second? Probably the flashy threads she likes to sew into her pants. Definitely the way her body put weight on right around its center before it thought about adding some anywhere else. It was the very reason Thomas didn't want to have kids. Most men would probably worry about their lifestyle changing when kids come on scene, but Thomas was worried that her body would go through what is essentially a war with itself to produce an heir, giving up its tight borders for the softness of motherhood. The absence of life blooming from her is suddenly very evident. She'd always thought of herself as someone who would have a family, but she had allowed her desires to be flattened into the slow rolling wheels of Thomas's superficial concerns. Who was he to be superficial, anyway? Why did she ever agree to that? Her own weakness, the willingness to give up every bit of self to preserve the couple, is beginning to glare through as darkly as the things Ann overlooked about Thomas.

So her midsection got a little thicker. Did Thomas read that as permission to take up with someone else? And damn, her legs were looking good from all that Zumba and her middle was slowly shrinking back to what it was a few years ago, but he hadn't even been home enough to notice.

Ann Without turns her gaze back across the café to inspect the other Anne, who is picking at a pile of fries drizzled with cheese sauce that arrived a moment ago, causing their conversation to stop while Thomas shoves a burger in his face. Ann Without adds Thomas's atrocious table manners to the list of things she's overlooked.

Anne with an *e* looks nice, but more a hair shirt than fur coat kind of woman, the kind just like Ann Without who would sacrifice herself to keep Thomas. Thomas really has a type. Anne looks like someone with simple goals who would search for her dream home among a sea of identical floorplans and paint jobs in a development called Déjà View Estates and never see the irony. A girl who was holding out for a rock star in her twenties but, now pushing thirty, ends up settling for a part-time master of the bongos. She looks innocent enough that she might march unknowingly right up to death's door and ask to borrow a cup of sugar. She's an inexperienced gardener who plants what she thinks will be a towering sunflower but instead a vining hybrid squash grows from the soil and produces warty fruit that tastes . . .

Ann Without is yanked from her thoughts by the realization that Anne With has stood up suddenly, letting her polite napkin fall from her lap and onto the floor, an action she seems not to notice as she turns and hurries across the diner to the back hall with blank silhouettes of a triangular skirted woman and a blocky man above the doorway. The neon sign above has burned out its "rest," leaving "rooms" glowing red against the pasty wall.

Ann Without is relieved that her husband's back is to her, so he won't see her grab her purse and follow Anne With into the bathroom.

As the heavy door sighs closed on its long hinge, Ann Without sees that there are only two stalls and one is already closed. Water drips into the single sink, tapping a spot that has darkened from years of this same drip slowly weakening the clean porcelain surface and leaving it stained. She steps through the open stall door and tries to figure out a reasonable position to assume in the confined space as she works out why she followed Anne in here in the first place. She sets paper on the seat and sits with her pants still up and her purse on her lap.

In the next stall, a trickling sound gives way to silence. But only for a few seconds.

"No . . . no no nonononono . . ."

Anne With is whispering frantically. The toilet paper dispenser spins around and around. In the ensuing silence, Ann Without thinks she hears the labored breathing of someone holding back sobs.

Thomas would hate to hear this. Not because he empathizes with someone who is in pain and suffers alongside them with a supportive—if obligatory—arm around the shoulders, but because he dreads the lasso that someone else's pain in his vicinity drops around him, dragging him like a helpless calf to the branding iron into helping another human sort out their emotions. She almost giggles at the image of Thomas with his arms pinned to his sides by the tightening rope of Anne's upset here in the bathroom.

Ann Without waits silently as Anne With pulls her sobs under control and commences with sniffling, enough that Ann Without can tell the other Anne's nose is dripping at a higher speed than her body can manage on its standard breathing schedule. Ann Without wonders why Anne With doesn't just wad up a tad of that ream of toilet paper she's just unleashed and use it as tissue for her nose.

What feels like a very long time ticks by, marked by the persistent drips landing in the sink every few seconds and the periodic sniffs from Anne With. Ann Without shifts her legs and weight to make it sound like something legitimate is happening in her stall. She pulls at the toilet paper theatrically, then folds it carefully back over and over itself to rest on top of the roll, knowing no one will ever use this because it's already been touched. She thinks about ripping off a few squares and suggestively pretending to blow her nose into it. But why would Ann want to help this woman who is having lunch with *her* husband and tracing love circles onto his leg under the table?

Rummaging commences in Anne With's stall. It pauses, then continues at a more frantic pace.

"Do you have a tampon?"

The way she keeps getting lost in her own head makes Ann Without like a nervous fawn alone in the woods today, because she jumps again at the question and the hand that appears beneath the partition.

Aha! Anne with an *e* doesn't have everything after all. Ann Without considers the small, lightly calloused and very utilitarian hand open and asking under the metal divider. She thinks about the battered-wrapper tampon lying somewhere at the bottom of her own purse. The kind every woman has unless she is past the time of fruitful delights or is in fruit at the moment and doesn't need one for a long time.

"Eh, no, sorry."

The words quietly escape her mouth, lingering on the *noooooo*, before she has a chance to ratify the final bill of sale this statement represents. She's shut down the possibility of conversation before she even decided whether she wanted to talk to Anne.

The hand pulls back to its side and disappears. The unfurling of yards of toilet paper begins again. Ann Without is certain Anne With has pulled sufficient paper out to float away on her own tissue raft.

After Anne With has passed so many minutes of stuffing and rustling in the next stall that Ann Without's legs have gone a shade of numb just shy of cold dead stone, there is a semi-triumphant completion to a zip in Anne With's stall that sounds strained against what it means to contain, and then a pause before the feet turn around to face the toilet.

Ann Without feels her ears tense in preparation for the assault of sound she expects from the imminent flush and its echoes off the hard surfaces that surround the capsules that contain the two Ann(e)s together, yet apart. Instead, a cavernous silence beats its nothingness against her eardrums and the drip from the sink sounds louder than before. Its rhythmic tick . . . tick . . . tick marks seconds that threaten to turn into minutes and Anne With hasn't moved. Neither, accordingly, has Ann Without.

The sole of her shoe squeaks quietly against the polished concrete floor as Ann Without leans forward to peer under the divider. She sees the deep plum flats that Anne With chose to meet her lover in and Ann Without can't disagree with this choice. They're very cute shoes. Just as Ann has to brace a hand against the metal door to stop herself from falling onto the floor, from the stall next to her the slowest flush she has ever heard from a public toilet begins to swirl and finishes with an echoing roar.

The latch slides open and the plum flats walk haltingly out of the stall. As the sound of water filling the bowl subsides, Ann Without hears faint beeps being dialed. The bathroom's rigid surfaces echo even the sound of the phone ringing on the other end until a click and a cartoonishly distant voice picks up.

"Momma, I'm not pregnant anymore," Anne With whispers into the phone.

A wail tremolos through the phone but is quickly drowned out by Anne With keening through clenched teeth until she gets her tears under control. The voice on the other end makes noises that lilt upward at the end in a question and Anne With answers in a shaky whisper.

"I know," she shudders into the phone, "we only figured it out last week." She draws a shaky breath. "He was going to leave her because of it. But now . . ." Her words trail off into wet sounds somewhere between moaning and weeping.

Somewhere far beyond what Ann Without considers her world, a great tilting jolts her sideways and out of earshot of the conversation outside her stall door. The cold of the porcelain she sits on that has crept into her deadened legs flashes into her core and freezes Ann in place. The planet's spin, the way life courses around each being's movement, is suddenly very evident to her stopped body. The stagnation of her own life, the pause of her body's patterns and desires so that she could wrap her existence around Thomas, becomes a looming wall that she never saw until this moment when she has left that reality to enter an unrecognized space in the café restroom where she sits fully clothed on a toilet she doesn't need with her husband's lover on the other side of the thin metal partition.

She knew. Anne with an *e* knew about her.

The Anne outside the stall door continues making noises and eventually ends her conversation. The Ann inside the stall feels her dizziness pass and hugs the leather purse on her lap to her chest as an anchor to keep herself tied to the cold surfaces of this reality.

Ann Without listens to the faucet spray water into the sink and overtake the sounds of Anne With sniffling. Good. Let her wash away what is on her hands. The paper towel dispenser grates and after a few minutes of dabbing sounds, the door hisses open and groans back closed.

This time, in the new silence, the muffled sobs come from Ann. Ann without a husband or a child or even any dignity left.

The shrapnel of her previous existence settles onto the unforgiving white tiles around her. The purple threads down the outside of her third-favorite jeans, the ones she altered to get Thomas to look at her again, burn into her skin. The lazy naivete they represent weighs against her legs. It was never about what she did to get noticed—he was never going to see her fitness, the thread in her jeans, or the style of her hair. He might not even know to this day whether her name has the flourish of an *e* on the end of it or not.

Ann Without rummages through her purse for the nail clippers that roll around the bottom somewhere with the unoffered tampon. The folded metal tool lands in her hand with a satisfying chill, and this satisfaction grows as she uses it to snip open and tear at the end of the purple threads on the hem of her pants. As she pulls at the loops higher and higher, the jeans bell open wide from her ankle to her knee. The threads stop at her knees, and so does she. This movement has brought the blood rushing back into her legs and she rises to her feet with the ends of her pants swaying loosely around them.

The chill she felt from the porcelain has drifted into her chest and formed a knot there. She wads the purple threads into a similar tangle and digs through her purse for the tampon. Then she wrestles off the ring Thomas bought, the smallest diamonds available at the jeweler that day she still remembers with a warm glow that is quickly fading in a new clarity that allows Ann Without to see that their excitement was really only hers and Thomas had just been along for the ride. The stones had long ago stopped glinting in even the brightest light. She pushes the ring against the tampon, but it won't fit around the wrapper and applicator. Once she removes those, the gold band slides effortlessly over the cotton bundle. It looks much better there, on the plain white wadding with its little braided mouse tail. There is a strange relief in recognizing that fighting to stay married to

Thomas is no more effective than harvesting snow. It's just making her cold with no yield.

Purple ball with tampon and ring wadded into her fist and her third-favorite jeans now flatteringly tight around her thighs and swinging widely around her ankles, Ann Without strides from the bathroom and back out into the brightly lit restaurant. She's already halfway across the room of tables when Anne With, seated back next to Thomas, looks up and her eyes grow wide as the pieces fall into place in her mind, as though the growing acknowledgment is too much for her cranium to contain. Thomas turns in response and leaps out of his chair when he sees his wife.

"Ann(e)!" Both with an *e* and without.

Two Ann(e)s look back at him. It's the most animated Ann has ever seen her husband and the look on his face is one she'll remember for a long time to come: a sudden swarm of details and lies and realizations like so many biting flies he can't wave away. A shiver of delight at his surprise and discomfort thrills her spine and motivates her forward to their table where the congealing remains of their lunch lie in puddles of their own seepage. She doesn't bother looking at the other Anne's face because she knows the pain already etched into the space between her carefully cultivated brows.

Keeping her eyes locked onto Thomas's to glean more satisfaction from his shock, Ann unfurls her hand to reveal the messy nest of purple threads with the dull shine of her ring on its white carriage in the center.

"You might need this."

The pile rolls from her palm to land with a muffled metallic clunk next to Thomas's plate, the end of the tampon string dipped into a spot of ketchup. Perfect.

She spins and marches toward the light pouring through the glass front door, dropping a five next to her half-full chipped mug on her way past, and revels in the silence at the table where Anne with an *e* and Thomas stare after her. Ann without an *e* thought Anne with an *e* had everything. She was wrong about so many things, but of one idea she is sure, and this thought propels her out into the sunshine. Ann is better without.

Maintenance

Kristina Van Sant

He raked the late October leaves,
slender as desiccated parrots,
into three predictable piles
(connect the dots from compost heap to raker)

before he left, one last act of domestic integrity,
then propped his rusty rake against the front
door frame, clambered into his loaded Pinto
and drove off while his handiwork dispersed

across the windy yard. She touched
none of it, left the rake to freeze, weld
itself to the house in December.
Snow cover loiters into March, then melts,

leaves the careful landscaping mucky, treacherous.
She waits until sun curdles mud, then rakes up
the leaf clumps, dry crust but sodden inside.
Most of the first good day is taken up

with this task. Muscles in her back, arms, thighs
thicken, grow strong. She lifts loads by flipping
her rake over, sliding its staggered tines between
earth and leaves, and steadying every collected lump

she then rises with her other hand's slight pressure
resting on top. Underneath, beetles and bisected
worms drop from each leafy mass. She dumps
the last cluster onto the chicken wire rounded heap,

watches the insects wriggle down, ready to nudge
the compost along. She locks the rake in the toolshed
and heads for the house, stopping halfway to stretch,
blistered fingers reaching towards the sun.

My Old Kentucky Home

Ellen Pauley Goff

DELLA MADE THE MISTAKE OF GLANCING DOWN AT THE EMAIL THAT PINGED onto her laptop screen at the exact moment the guy sitting next to her in lecture leaned over and asked if she wanted to go out this weekend. The email was from her parents, who were halfway around the world on a cruise ship filled with enough shrimp cocktail to entertain a gaggle of empty nesters.

Della's Great-Aunt Pearl had died. The funeral was in just three days and they would not make it back, so could Della make the six-hour drive from Chicago to Louisville to pick up her grandmother? Someone needed to drive Grandma Faye to southern Kentucky for her sister's funeral since she couldn't be trusted with a machine for more than an hour at a time. Della suppressed an audible groan and instead settled on a whispered, exasperated, "*Lord.*"

She loved her grandmother. That was not the predicament. No one, however, had been enamored with Great-Aunt Pearl, except perhaps her husband Jeb, who passed only a few months ago himself. Although in southern Kentucky, where bales of hay outnumbered bodies, people often settled with whomever they could find.

Bam, there was that unnamable feeling that appeared when she thought about things like the sprawling yet still isolated suburbs unique to rural areas, or the drawl she slipped into on the phone with relatives, or her high school parking lot, or really just parking lots in general, which were nearly always a sign of expansion but never growth.

"That's a no, then?" the guy next to her whispered back.

Della glanced at him. He was not just any boy, unfortunately. Li had black hair and brown eyes, and his sockets were set so far back and beneath his matching dark brows that he had the appearance of staring through layers of atmosphere you didn't know you were breathing.

She did want to go out with him. She *really* wanted. They were both seniors and had ended up next to each other in the fourth row of their Shakespeare class every day since the start of the semester. She wasn't sure if this unabashed, direct approach of his was a theater-major thing, but it was certainly a refreshing one on a college campus where guys were just as coy and vague as the flighty older southern women she knew.

The words were out of her mouth before she realized how bad they would sound. "My great-aunt died. I have to drive to Kentucky tomorrow."

Li smiled. "You can just tell me no. I'll listen."

"I'm serious. I'll have to miss classes Friday and rent a car. My grandma needs me to drive her to the funeral."

"In Louisville?"

Lord. He remembered. Another pang of disappointment struck her. He was accumulating points faster than she could appreciate them. "A couple hours south of it. Almost to Tennessee. Maybe we could do something when I get back?" If he were still interested, that is.

He turned away from her. After a pause that was long enough for Della to decide *that was that,* there would be no Li for her, he turned back. "Need company?"

"What?"

He shrugged. "I like road trips."

"It's a funeral."

"I'll help drive."

A sudden image stuck in her head: Li, with his pale skin and black hair, in the cab of a pickup truck, squished between guys with names like Bud and Cody and shotguns as long as their chests were across. She had the sudden urge to run out of the lecture hall to the nearest bathroom so she could scream and pee a little.

"You're serious," she said.

"Pick me up on Friday," he replied. "I'll hang my suit in the shower to steam out the wrinkles."

GRANDMA FAYE LOVED HER family very much. There was nothing and no one above kin.

However, after the many years she had spent on this earth, sometimes kin grew tiresome. No one gets to choose their siblings, and Faye and her sister Pearl made some good years and ruined other years. Pearl had been the troublemaker in their family, Faye the baby of all the children and thus the angel. Another sister had been the studious one, a younger brother had been cunning, an older brother had been the true father figure. With Pearl gone, Faye was the last one left. Perhaps now she would have to inhabit all of these roles.

As Faye watched her granddaughter pull into her condo's driveway Friday afternoon, she was more happy to see Dellanne than she was sad about Pearl. That's what happened with time. She had not become less sentimental. At her age, it was hard to be surprised, and when it was hard to be surprised, it was difficult to be sad. In truth, she made a bet with her hidden stash of cash that Pearl would've gone foul a long time ago, what with her sister's smoking habit. No, she was not very sad. And she owed her cookie jar fifty dollars.

"Dellanne!" she cried, meeting her granddaughter in the drive. No sooner had she wrapped her arms around her girl than a boy stepped out of the passenger side of the car. Oh Lord. He was a handsome one. With dimples, at that.

"Grandma, this is Li, a friend of mine. He wanted to come along."

Faye, like most elderly southerners, did not trust outsiders encroaching on family business. But she did appreciate a handsome face, especially one that reminded her of her husband when he had been alive and young. A little bit of Cary Grant if Cary Grant had been more like Elvis. She offered the two kids food since they were both thin and probably studied too much when they should have been eating. When they were ready to take off, Li moved his backpack from the front to the back seat without being asked so Faye could sit up front, and it was then that Faye knew she would not mind the drive with the young man.

Kin was a strange thing. As a young girl, she had grown up in the deep south of Kentucky where blood ran stronger—and more poisonous, sometimes—than moonshine. Yet, in a single instant, someone could be absorbed into the bubble that surrounded families for generations, and from that moment they were just as responsible for all of your secrets as you were for theirs.

GREAT-AUNT PEARL'S FARMHOUSE was a handful of miles off a dirt road that was itself a handful of miles off a main road that ran through a thimble of a town just north of the border between Kentucky and Tennessee.

It was still light, and Grandma Faye insisted they go up to the house first. Now that Pearl had passed, no one was living there, and Faye wanted to make sure a relative had done their part and closed up the place while folks waited for the funeral. The house sat on two hundred acres of good farmland that belonged to Faye and Pearl's side of the family, not Jeb's. Faye also wanted to drive around the property to make sure all looked well and good. By right, it was all hers now.

The farmhouse blazed with light when Della steered the car off the dirt road and onto the gravel drive. There were no fewer than five pickup trucks parked next to the house. The entire drive from Louisville, Li's eyes stuck to the rolling bluegrass and the small towns that were shy behind their churches. He answered questions from Grandma Faye, every so often giving a quick tug to a wayward strand of Della's hair when the old woman wasn't looking. Della met his eyes many times in the rearview mirror. But out of everything Della caught him staring at, she could tell this cavalry of Chevys, Fords, and Dodges was something he had never seen before in San Francisco where his parents lived, or in Hong Kong where his grandparents were.

"What. In. The. World." Grandma Faye said, eyeing the active house. "Lord, can't trust no one to do things properly down here. I don't even recognize these cars. Here, park right here. They've gone and done blocked the whole drive."

As her grandma made like a demon for the front door, Della scrambled out of the car to catch up. The presence of strangers could certainly light a fire under the older woman's ass.

Li jumped out, his eyes alight as he circled the trucks, automobiles ever the common language between men and cultures. "What does everyone carry around in these anyway? Do you all really need to haul stuff all the time? This thing's massive!" he said, kicking the tire of the nearest truck in admiration.

Good question, Della thought. Then she noticed the odd, irregular outline of shapes in the trucks' beds. That was . . . that was a lamp. That was a rocking chair in another. One truck's bed was filled with entire racks of what appeared to be moth-eaten flannels. And Della was pretty sure if she lifted up the tarp in the bed closest to her, she would find Pearl's perpetually out of tune Wurlitzer stand piano. The trucks were full of junk. *Pearl and Jeb's stuff.*

That feeling flushed through her again, and she could begin to pinpoint what it was, at least on the surface: a fear of something, of an outcome yet to blow through. It made her stomach queasy in the way it sometimes felt in the morning when she hadn't eaten anything yet and so the acid in her gut was strong and hungry. It wasn't really fear of things like pickup trucks and old lamps and funerals for people no one liked—but it was close.

The door must have been unlocked, because Faye was already in the house by the time Della and Li scrambled up to the front porch.

It was not quite a party, but because an open container of Moon Pies was sitting on a coffee table—one of the few pieces of furniture left—it might as well have been in Faye's eyes. Everyone in the den and kitchen was too busy to notice the trio at first. What Della assumed were distant cousins were hauling away furniture, removing decorations and pictures from walls to reveal the less-faded wallpaper beneath, and packing trash bags of linens into boxes stamped with a logo that said *Brookside Baptist Church*.

"Don't sit anywhere," Della said to Li when he moved toward a couch. "They kept their loaded guns underneath the cushions." He moved a little closer to her instead.

Faye darted from room to room, suddenly ten years more nimble as she weaved around folks. She was searching. Or hunting, Della wasn't sure. Li was munching on a Moon Pie when she looked behind her to make sure he had not been swallowed up in the disarray.

"Ms. Faye!" a voice screeched from the kitchen. Della and her grandmother whirled to face an older woman with a bob of dyed cotton candy pink hair the box had likely promised was supposed to be a soft rose. "Well look at you, I haven't seen you in ages!"

Faye gave the woman a tight-lipped smile that Della knew was reserved for people she did not like or did not know, which were usually the same thing.

"Don't you remember me? Sissy from Hill Ridge High. We were in the same class."

Recognition spilled onto Faye's face only to fall away as a frown shoved in. It appeared Faye did, in fact, remember Sissy.

"What's going on, Sissy?" Faye asked, looking around pointedly at the flutter of activity in a house that should have remained respectfully empty until after the funeral.

Sissy cocked her pink head. "What do you mean? We're just clearing out a few things before the funeral. It's what Pearl had asked for when she knew she was getting sicker. I volunteered to help take care of these things for her after she passed."

"What kind of things?" Faye pressed. It was hard to tell if Sissy's evasion was anything more than just spaciness as a by-product of a mind cluttered with years of tobacco smoke.

"Things like clothes and blankets." She nodded to a group of cousins hauling a box through the front door. "She asked me to donate them to the church. With a number of other things. Pearl was such a good soul. Never wanted anything to go to waste."

Faye narrowed her eyes as Della's mouth unhinged slightly. "My sister," Faye began very slowly, "asked you to *donate* something to the church. For nothing in return."

Sissy's head bobbed. "Well, yes! We run a drive every month. Collecting clothes and furniture and kitchen supplies and such. She wanted to donate most everything here. My husband is the preacher, and I can tell you the church will so appreciate this."

Faye and Della were speechless. Sissy's smile grew each second Faye said nothing. Della looked back to see Li, sans Moon Pie, but now holding a box someone had dropped into his arms while folks loaded Pearl's collection of kitschy salt and pepper shakers into it. She gave him a look and he gave her a sheepish shrug in return that was both a defense and a cry for help.

Faye found her voice by the time Li managed to abandon the box and join them. "So, how much exactly is she giving away here, Sissy?" she asked.

Sissy's expression slipped. "I think you best just come to the reading of the will tomorrow. It's all laid out there. Pearl was very generous."

"Generous? I don't remember this in her will."

"She updated it before she passed," Sissy explained, like this was the most normal thing in the world. "And so did Jeb, before he was called away. Pearl and I have always been close as schoolgirls. I helped them make all the arrangements in the end."

Faye nodded. "I'm sure you did."

Sissy took the awkward pause that followed to finally glance at Della. "Dellanne, I hardly recognized you. Look at you, all grown up, a real woman. Where in the world did you get that blonde hair from?" She nodded to Faye, whose hair was almost as dark as Li's, even before she had to start dyeing it. She faced Li. "I'm Sissy. You look more like Faye's grandbaby than anyone here." She extended her hand.

Li gave Sissy's outstretched hand such an intense look as was his nature that it became obvious to everyone that he was seriously debating about whether to take it. After a pause, he stuffed his hands into his armpits.

Faye puffed out her chest as Sissy withered a fraction. "We'll be there tomorrow. This is all too fast. I'm Pearl's kin, after all."

"Yes, well," Sissy tittered, a shrill laugh caught in her throat. "We're trying to honor their wishes. We can't change the wills now, can we?" she asked in a way that suggested there had most certainly been an opportune time to change them.

Faye turned to leave, wiggling her hand into the nook of Li's elbow on her left and into Della's on her right. Her eye landed on something in the corner and the trio stopped abruptly like some confused circus act on their way to the stage.

"Sissy," Faye called over her shoulder. "Where is that going?"

Sissy followed her gaze. In the corner sat a large print of the traditional 1958 *My Old Kentucky Home* painting by Haddon Sundblom. The print was nearly the size of the fridge and had to be fifty years old by itself; its brass frame was now more tarnish than brass.

"That?" Sissy asked. "It'll be moved and stored at my house until we figure out where it's supposed to go. The reading tomorrow will shed some light on some of the miscellaneous items. It's an awfully gorgeous picture, though."

"Pearl told me she was giving that to me. It was our mother's."

"I suppose we'll find out tomorrow, won't we?"

Faye pointed at the painting and looked Sissy squarely in the face. "That belongs to me."

They left before they saw the beginnings of Sissy's defiant and slightly fearful expression. When they were on the porch and in the quiet once more, Grandma Faye's shoulders sagged a centimeter as she said, in a softer voice this time, "That belongs to me."

FAYE STARED HOLES INTO her hot brown. It was a pitiful thing, the ham tough and the gravy watery and devoid of salt. She could have made one *miles* better. But she chided herself. Who was she to judge the diner's food when she didn't live around here any longer and thus had no claim to opinions on the town's makings and doings? That's what happened when you left a place. For a while, you could return and still call yourself a stitch in the community quilt. For a while, you could come back and still be party to the gossip, you could still contribute a marshmallow salad recipe to the church's cookbook.

But Faye had left this little town for Louisville such a long time ago that her sister would have told her she didn't even have the right to say its name.

Maybe Pearl was right. But Faye was at least owed that goddamned painting.

Boop's Diner was the only late-night eatery in town, which meant nine o'clock and not a minute later. They had come from the reading of the will, which took place at—where else, damn Sissy and her claws—Brookside Baptist Church down the road from the farmhouse. Dellanne and Li sat across from her in the booth, both of them watching her with tentative expressions as if she were about to call down a lightning storm. The reading, of course, had been a disaster. Forget the lamps and the rugs and the bed skirts and the jewelry and the guns and the television and the china cabinets and the tractors.

They were taking the house and the farm.

A week before his death, Jeb had changed his will to ensure Pearl inherited everything he owned. The two of them never had any children, but his cousins and distant relatives had been cut out. Sissy had shown up on Pearl's doorstep only a few weeks before Jeb passed first. Pearl, seeing only a simple woman offering to drive her to doctors' appointments and run errands, gave in easily, no longer the spitfire Faye knew as her older sister. Faye couldn't have cared less about this, except for the fact that Pearl did the exact same thing. A week before Pearl's death, her newfound friend Sissy helped her redo her will. Everything she owned—including the farmhouse and the land it sat on—she was giving to the church.

But what set Faye's blood to boiling more than anything was Sissy had convinced both Jeb and Pearl to be baptized before they passed. Baptized! Her sister, dressed in white with her head sunk beneath the water of the creek that ran behind the farm? She wanted to spit. Her sister was more likely to drown the preacher himself than take an interest in God. She snorted.

Della and Li looked up at the sound, their burgers half demolished in front of them. The kids kept staring at her, but Faye didn't mind because she was watching them just as much. It provided her a little bit of escape in this mess. She had not been around a young man since her daughter dated Della's father. And before that, she married her own husband when she was barely eighteen and thus never spent much time courting anyone else. It was some kind of comfort to see boys still moved the same pieces across the same board. Li had a habit of leaning toward Della. It was clear the boy just wanted to be in Della's space, to be noticed and accounted for. Well, she couldn't blame him for that. Didn't they all want the same thing?

Faye's mind wandered. How was it, having stayed behind and never left the state, Faye led quite a happy life—but that, at the same time, Della flew away as soon as she could and still had found someone? Weren't she and her grandbaby of the same blood, made of the same stuff? How could a single generation between them lead to such different people?

"Grandma? You done? We should head out."

Faye came back to herself. Her granddaughter looked worried, but then again, the girl always looked a little worried these days, and it doubled like rising biscuit dough when she came back home. It would be hard to live in two places, to have one foot planted in a city and one planted in the absence of one. Poor child.

Della's eyes found something behind Faye's head, and Faye turned to see what had caused the urgent need to leave. Sissy had pulled into the diner's parking lot. In Jeb's old truck. A young blond boy with a few other fellows jumped out with her and picked a booth on the other side of the diner. After they finished reading Pearl's will, Faye had stormed out to get the kids some supper instead of confronting Sissy head-on. But she had flipped the old pink woman the bird and did not care if Sissy or God had seen it.

Faye nodded to Della. But before they could leave, the blond boy and his sunburned friends strolled over and planted themselves at the edge of each side of the booth.

"I'm Casey," said the blond boy, who looked about Della's age but did not have the expression of worry that most intelligent people had. "Sissy's grandson, Ms. Faye. Pleased to meet all of y'all." He did not offer his hand. "Dellanne," he said, nodding and using her name as if he knew her, and Faye was pretty sure he did not. The people down here liked to use names before they had been given, as if to say they could own something without asking.

With Della by the window, Li was at eye level with the pistol strapped to Casey's hip. He nodded at the boys. "I'm Li. We were actually just leaving."

A boy in the back hollered "Rush Hour!" causing Casey and the others to crack up.

"That was Jackie Li, right?" Casey added. "Or Jet Chan?"

Li's stare went blank, head swiveling slowly to face Della, like he was in disbelief rather than offended. Della knew, if there were a moment in time when Li would give up, cards folded, and throw himself into the nearest coal-polluted backwater creek to avoid her—this would be that moment. But he stayed and simply stole one of her remaining fries, so Della followed his lead and kept quiet even though her fingers itched to make chicken scratch out of Casey's face.

"A shame about today," Casey continued. "Pearl shouldn't have done you like that, Ms. Faye, but I suppose someone's connection to God and their church is stronger than kin sometimes. Nana Sissy wanted me to make sure you knew you're always welcome at our house. We got plenty of space. And the church'll do something good with Pearl's house. Don't worry."

"Where's *My Old Kentucky Home*? Ask your Nana about that," Faye said.

Casey's sunburned forehead crinkled as his eyebrows rose. "She didn't tell you? The church'll be auctioning off some stuff from the house. Pearl's—"

"Pearl's wishes, yes, we know," Faye finished.

"We'll be helping a lot of people in town with the money we raise, Ms. Faye."

"Enjoy the truck," Faye said sweetly.

Casey didn't acknowledge the bite to Faye's words and just smiled. As his friends sauntered back across the diner to join Sissy and her husband the preacher, he tipped an imaginary hat at Li. "Later, Jet Chan."

That was it. Della snatched the nearest fork in her fist, not yet quite sure what kind of damage she intended to inflict with said fork, but Li beat her to it. He rose like he was going to be a gentleman and offer his hand to Casey to say goodbye, but before Della could blink, Li grabbed the ketchup bottle and squirted a large *Li* right onto the front of Casey's John Deere T-shirt. Even the dot made it in there.

"It's *Jet Li*," Li corrected him.

Everyone was silent, looks of mild horror popping onto faces across the diner. Then Casey woke up. He landed one swift punch across Li's nose, but only one. A couple local cops were sitting a few booths over and quickly yanked Casey back so Faye and Della could pull a bleeding Li from the diner.

The cops' grumbling followed them from the diner, they'd let this one go just this once since everyone was grieving in their own way, even though them two boys couldn't've known Great-Aunt Pearl that well really, bless her heart, and . . .

As Faye left the diner, Sissy waved goodbye from the safety of her booth.

DELLA WOKE HERSELF UP at midnight. Restlessness helped pull her awake, a decision that needed finishing, one she had started to make when she saw Sissy pull up in Jeb's truck. Or maybe it wasn't a decision but rather that odd feeling again, one that seemed like something close to fear but that did not kindly offer up what it was she needed to be afraid of.

She crawled out of bed, moving like a slug to avoid waking Grandma Faye next to her. The motel they were in was just on the edge of town as all motels were. No way would Faye have taken any of the neighbors' offers to house them for the weekend; they were all in bed with Sissy, as far as her grandmother was concerned.

Her feet bare on the crusty carpet, Della padded over to the other double bed where Li was sleeping. His nose had not been broken, but dried blood still stuck in his cupid's bow. She gave his shoulder a shake. His eyes popped right open, almost too fast.

"Were you waiting for me to sneak over here in the middle of the night?" she asked in a hushed whisper.

A pause. "Yes."

"Even after the diner? I'm sorry about Casey. About all of it. Down here—"

He waved a hand. "I just wish I could've seen you use that fork." A wink.

She would tuck that away for later. "Get dressed," she said, grabbing the rental car keys off the top of the mini fridge.

"Where are we going?" he asked, but he was already slipping his jeans over his boxers, like he had been planning for this scenario just as much as the former one.

* * *

THEY PARKED THE RENTAL car at the bottom of the drive to Sissy's house, which, because it was also the preacher's house, was built next door to Brookside Baptist Church. Della and Li sat in the quiet car for several minutes just staring up at the church and the house, which were both dark and seemingly empty. But Della knew Sissy was in there, asleep and content.

Li's voice was a shot in the stillness. "What's so special about this painting anyway? Isn't it a print that could just be replicated?"

Della didn't know. But it had been Faye's mother's, which meant it had become one of those heirlooms that absorbed value on the basis of how long it had taken up space in a living room. She said, "They won't have locked any doors. No one does around here. We'll grab it, go to the funeral tomorrow, and then be back to Louisville before Sissy realizes it's gone."

"And why can't we just slip out and steal it during the service?"

"Sissy would know what we were doing the moment we left the room."

Li nodded, agreeing. "What if they're awake?"

"It's not in the house. Casey said it's in the auction so it's stashed in the church." She was not completely positive about this, but Li didn't need to know that.

"So, we're going to break in and steal something from a church?" he repeated. He let out a low whistle. She remembered then that he had been raised Catholic. "I must like you," he teased.

She strained to study his features in the dark car. "I just want to be clear here," she began. "I'm not going to have sex with you just because you came all the way down here for the funeral, not even if you help me steal this thing."

He grinned, a joke in his smile. "Well shit, that was my whole plan."

An absurd giggle escaped her at the sarcasm in his voice. Her eyes flew back to Sissy's house and then to the trucks in the driveway.

A second giggle died in her throat when her gaze landed on Jeb's truck. Fury burned in her cheeks. "Uncle Jeb—Pearl's husband—taught me to shoot, you know," she said, not to anyone in particular.

The fear appeared then, stronger this time, like the bite of vinegar in her grandmother's coleslaw. And then she realized what the fear was for, why she always felt like a bad cold, or a bout of food poisoning, was coming on when she thought of going home. She liked this world just enough to stay. And whether *home* home was way down here, or if it meant Louisville, it really didn't matter. All it took was one good trip, and then another, and then you were coming back all the time after you worked so hard to leave and it was doable because it was comfortable and the comfort is what scared her the most. Before you knew it, you had taken five steps forward just to take five back again and it was up to the next generation to make the progress in the end. You had wasted your chance.

"Why do they stay?" she said into the darkness.

Li tilted his head at her. "Why do we leave?" She hadn't expected an answer and at her confused expression, he went on. "Why do people like us leave? We're the only children, the last of the line, so to speak. Oldest children leave without any guilt because they know their parents will still have their siblings for a while. And youngest children leave because they've watched their siblings do it all before and their parents are used to it. So why do *we* leave?"

She didn't have an answer. Honestly, she had forgotten he was an only child, too; maybe that was why he had been so excited to come with her for company and why she had been so eager to accept. Who sits shotgun with you when everyone in your family is either miles ahead up the road already or miles behind you on the trip.

Without speaking, they were out of the car and shuffling toward the church, their hoods thrown over their heads. The doors were unlocked and the painting was there like she prayed it would be. They found it leaning against a rocking chair in the nursery tucked at the back of the sanctuary, with other items for the auction strewn around amid stuffed animals and forgotten pacifiers. With Li on one side and Della on the other, they hauled the painting into the crooks of their waists and then hauled ass out of the church.

But Della had not accounted for the dogs.

Apparently Sissy had three massive bloodhounds living in their backyard, dogs that had all come awake upon hearing Della and Li. Their howls broke the silence and lights flickered on immediately in the house.

Della and Li ran, bolting for the car, the painting jostling between them. She thought for sure the glass over the print would break at any moment and then they would be leaving a sparkling trail of broken guilt for Sissy to find. More lights came on but faded quickly in the darkness around the house so that they stumbled across the shadowy and pocketed earth in front of them. She cringed as their shoes crunched the gravel, the sound filling her ears like gunshots until, from the house, came actual gunshots.

The stout sound of a healthy shotgun cut through the air.

"*Fuck,*" Li cursed under his breath.

They were steps from the rental car. Another shot broke the silence. Shrill voices echoed from the house now, probably Sissy calling 911. Li cursed again except this time in Cantonese.

They reached the car just as Della thought her chest would split. She started the engine as Li hefted the painting into the trunk and then he was beside her in the passenger seat, his hands braced on the dash. Another shot echoed behind them. Someone had spotted the car. She only hoped that the house was far enough away and the rental car an ambiguous enough shape and color that Sissy wouldn't be able to put two and two together.

Leaving the headlights off, they peeled away into the night.

FAYE SAT QUIETLY AS the funeral began, not uttering a single word of discontent. This was her sister's funeral, the only one she would get, so she needed to at least act respectable in front everyone. Being the only child left of the original siblings, she did not recognize many of the faces in the pews of Brookside Baptist Church that Sunday morning.

Faye sat quietly when the preacher, Sissy's husband, urged the guests to join him in singing hymns. They were hymns Pearl would have hated if she had ever listened to hymns. Sitting between Dellanne and Li, Faye simply hummed along with the words and latched onto her granddaughter's hand.

Faye sat quietly when Pearl's friends stood up and talked about what a fixture Pearl had been in the community. She only pursed her lips. The preacher asked if she wanted to say a few words as well, but she declined. There was nothing she needed to say in front of these people, and a small part of her was only just beginning to realize she was angry at Pearl for signing it all away. To people like Sissy, for that matter.

But when the time came for the preacher to speak about Pearl and the Christian life she had led under the protective eyes of God, Faye could no longer sit quietly.

"Our Pearl was the epitome of grace in this community," the preacher began. "Pearl had one of the kindest hearts I have ever known in a person. She showed compassion when others were aloof, empathy when others were envious, and goodness when others were angry. She lived and walked with Christ and we are a better people because of her. She and her husband were some of the most generous people—"

That was it. Faye stood and ambled up the aisle. It took a moment for everyone to notice her, and only when she reached the front of the sanctuary did the preacher shut his trap.

"Now hold on a minute," she said, staring out at the pews. "Y'all have no idea what you're talking about. My sister Pearl was no saint. She certainly wasn't a Christian. She did not volunteer; she did not willingly show up with donations in her arms. The only time she went to a food drive was to get free canned okra. None of you have any idea who she was and it's shameful. And she would have told every one of you that if she was here with us right now."

She took a steadying breath. The church had gone silent, and in the calm, she remembered why they were all here. Pearl was dead. She found Della's face in the crowd and held on. "She would have told you that if she was here," she repeated, softer this time.

Quickly—not because she was cold-hearted, but because she didn't like all those eyes on her—she kissed her thumb and touched it to Pearl's closed casket. Then she made for the front pew where Sissy sat and stood right in front of the darn woman with her pink hair.

Pointing one wrinkled finger at her, she said, "You, Sissy, Are. A. *Bitch*."

Faye was out the church before she could hear the gasps, Della and Li on her heels. Their stuff was already packed in the car. She folded herself into the passenger seat as Della got behind the wheel. No one said a word as the church appeared in the rearview mirror.

IT DID NOT TAKE Faye long to convince Li to stay for supper before the drive back to Chicago, and Della was soon to follow. The relieved smile that stole across her grandmother's face when they agreed made Della's heart hurt. *Of course* they could stay.

The ritual was familiar to Della. Only a few minutes in her grandmother's yellow-tiled kitchen, the ingredients for cornbread spread out on Formica countertops, and the muscle memory kicked in. Oil the skillet, mix the batter . . . Grandma Faye worked next to her, frying up chicken on the stovetop and then eventually kale and bacon in whatever the chicken left behind. Li was nearly crying in anticipation at the smell of butter and fried meat.

When supper was ready, Li helped Della carry the food to the long dining room table that was clearly meant for more than three people and that rested ambitiously in front of the fireplace. Faye arrived last, a basket of biscuits steaming under a dishtowel in her hands, and came to an abrupt stop when she rounded the corner into the dining room.

Della held her breath. Li gripped the back of a dining chair.

Propped up on the mantel of the fireplace was the stolen—repossessed—*My Old Kentucky Home* print.

They had not told Faye about it after sneaking back to the motel. If Sissy had asked Faye about it during the funeral, Della wanted her grandmother to be saved from lying in a church.

Faye just looked at the painting a long moment, absently setting the biscuits on the table. She did not ask how they got it back, or even if Sissy knew. She just stared, until finally she sank into a chair and began to cry.

Della hadn't ever seen her cry before. Not at any of the other siblings' funerals, and not over Pearl until that moment. Maybe it was because Pearl was the second-to-last sibling left. Faye was now next, if there were a line for these sorts of things. She thought about rubbing her grandmother's back, but she felt that was wholly inadequate. Truthfully, she didn't know how to comfort someone who had just arrived into a role she herself had been playing for two decades.

Li was clearly also itching to provide some comfort. He said, "I can hang it for you before we go if you've got a hammer."

Della didn't know why or how, but this did the trick. Grandma Faye wiped her cheeks and perked up, motioning for them to sit. "C'mon now, kids, let's eat. Food's getting cold. Thank you for my picture. I'll say grace."

They did as they were told and clasped hands. Li pinched Della's pinky as Faye prayed. For the rest of supper, *My Old Kentucky Home* looked down at them over the biscuits and ambrosia salad.

The Obituary I Wish I'd Written

Brooke Herter James

MY MOTHER REFUSED DOMESTICATION. SHE SEWED MY BROWNIE BADGE
on the right shoulder, which was the wrong shoulder. She put her
cigarettes out in the mashed potatoes on her dinner plate and called
for another Wild Turkey by wagging her finger up and down over the
lip of her highball glass. She spent an entire week saying
Supercalifragilisticexpialidocious instead of *Fuck*, and concluded that
saying *Fuck* was much more satisfying. She once reenacted *Christina's
World* by lying prone in our back field, arm stretched out in front of
her. She stayed in that pose for two hours, waiting for my father to
find her there. On my 13th birthday, she wrote EB White and
requested a letter, as it was his fault I was obsessed with pigs. He
obliged. For her 50th birthday, she requested that a boulder
resembling a harbor seal be moved from a Maine beach to the stream
in our suburban New York backyard. My father obliged. Then he left
her for a French woman with skinny ankles. My mother lay on the
couch for three days with a washcloth over her face and all the
curtains drawn, after which she announced that he never *did*
understand the difference between the *other side* and the *underside* of a
leaf. She never remarried. Instead, she flirted with a man who drove a
Subaru wagon with a volume of Shakespeare's sonnets on the backseat

> and on her gravestone
> at her request: *I am my*
> *own woman, well at ease*

To Helen and River of AA

Lila Quinn

and every woman
brave enough to mother
angry fuckers like me

I showed up dreaded
and shaved my head
within a week

a cliched cleansing
smoke haze rebirth
& requisite coffee

I bought for fifty cents
from sweet River
who tried to love me

like a sister, treated
me to pizza after my first
meeting & all I did

was cry and feel
like I wasn't ever
supposed to be here

like anywhere
men pulled focus
to themselves

but Helen, thirty-five years
sober and a kind of refined
I don't see in people

under 70, risked openly caring
for us all, especially the few
girls because we didn't

love ourselves yet
which made us almost
women. one day

I told her about
my feral child
scratching at my mind

the part of me
who hates people
prefers deer & coarse

fur of wild dogs
flowers fluttering
like hummingbird wings

and imitating
coyote howls, who wears
cuts and bruises like badges

I told her
I didn't know what to do
with this girl

like an exasperated
new mother beginning
to burst forth

in my psyche
as messy as a woman
like Helen would expect

doomed to love
the unruly children
we carry forever

apparently even
the ones who eventually
leave our bodies

desperate, half-crazed
and flirting with letting go
of the last love strong

as lilac in spring
that could ever make me
come to my sorrow-

dimmed senses and gently
I prayed, gently please
help me I was asking her

but not really I had no words
and thank god she'd
had children and raised them

knew in my frenzied
psychobabble
what I was saying

bring her with you
she said, *let her play*
in the corner

while we're in the meeting
look she said, pointing
to the corner full

of books and building blocks
in a little nook
just outside the circle

where we talked
about things my feral girl
doesn't want to understand

shouldn't have to understand
but does, is the thing
she had a great education

in how cruelty is made
is written into our bodies
pulls at our tangled

hair and slaps our face
leaves us to be taken
away from ourselves

his body inside me I didn't want
Helen knew
better than to punish her

or abandon her outside
knew she couldn't
ever be human without

other humans around
without learning
who can be trusted

and first on that list
had to be me, the part
of me that showed up

to that house in my neighborhood
where meetings happened
because two nights before

I'd downed several pitchers
of beer and swallowed
too much hydrocodone

because honestly
I didn't care
if my heart stopped

I still have the card
you gave me, Helen
it's the center

of a garland I made
out of letters people
mostly strangers

have given me
and this is how love
cradles us how any meeting

in love in any time or place
can keep us from drowning
in psychic wombs

we're meant to leave how else
can I take your hand & say
we will make it

To Auckland

Mellisa Pascale

AT THE AIRPORT, MY MOM HUGGED ME, MY DAD HUGGED ME, THEN MY MOM hugged me again (tighter this time), and after that they got in the car and drove away. I walked through the automatic doors and darted into the nearest bathroom to cry. When I had gotten on a plane to study in London three years previously, it tugged at me, but I knew when I'd see them again. This time I did not. This time, I did not have a return ticket.

I held it together until the plane took off, but on the six-hour flight to Los Angeles I alternately cried and stared into space. I was too bugged out to read the Neil Gaiman book I had just gotten for Christmas or to listen to Harry Styles or to eat the pocket-sized bag of trail mix I'd gotten in the airport. The woman next to me kindly pretended not to notice my on/off tears, perhaps assuming I was going back to college after winter break and having a rough time with it. *No, lady*, I wanted to say. *I am a real adult with a job and a car and school loan payments that I really try to keep up with. But then I decided I wanted to go backpacking in New Zealand.*

Imagining myself in New Zealand had been easy—lacing up my boots to go tramping in the backcountry or dipping a kayaking paddle into the azure waters of Abel Tasman National Park. However, imagining myself performing that act of departure, of *leaving*, had not actually crossed my mind. It was the fine print you skip over, the footnote you don't read.[1] The hideous thing about going to the airport and flying away is that you're leaving the entire time. Leaving your gate, leaving the runway, leaving your seat to wait in line for the bathroom, leaving the plane, leaving the airport, leaving wherever you went in order to go back to the airport because actually you just had a layover, and doing it all over again. Since I had planned a two-night stopover in Los Angeles, I would be leaving for three days before I made it to Auckland.

I thought that LA would be a bright, warm, and cheerful farewell to the US, which it was. So bright that, the morning after a restless night on an air mattress in a stranger's living room, the sun bounced off the buildings of downtown LA like a never-ending explosion that made my jet-lagged head split open in agony. So warm that anything discarded on the street—fries, spilt soda, wet cardboard—baked and rose from the pavement in a curdling perfume. So cheerful that every palm tree waved at me as though asking, "You all right?" *No*, I wanted to say. *I don't know when I'm going to see my dog again.*

While I did not possess the foresight to know that a stopover would be part of the *leaving* and not the *adventure*, I at least had something to distract me. Before I left, I had inquired about writing an article for a business travel website that I once interned for and was assigned an LA healthy travel guide. So, upon drawing the conclusion that there was nothing here appealing to me personally, I commenced some proper journalistic sleuthing. Mainly, I went for a walk in Elysian Park (where I would tell business travelers to run, of course) and found one of those fancy little juice bars with the word "cleanse" on their menu. Neighboring the juicery was a place that gave off serious pasta vibes, so I went in for some comfort food only to realize I had accidentally found a salad shop. This was great for the article, though not so great for my personal tastes. Since my stomach was nearing

---

[1] Please note that all *adventures* require *leaving*.

hour twenty-four of the stress-induced food strike I'd been on since leaving Philadelphia, I committed to the salad and sat down outside.

While shoving leaves in my mouth, I took out my tablet to start writing, simultaneously keeping an eye on the Pokémon GO app on my phone. I was a religious player at this period in my life. Anytime someone asked me why I was going to New Zealand, I delighted in telling them that I wanted to catch a rare Relicanth, which only spawns on the country's two main islands. To be clear, this was not my chief motivating factor, but it was always fun to see the blank look I got in return.

When a buzz from my phone revealed that an Abra had appeared, I lifted my index finger to fling a Pokéball. Immediately, someone shouted, "Catch anything good, nerd?"

Whipping around, I saw a guy two tables back notice me noticing him, whereupon he ceased waving at his approaching friend and said, "Sorry, didn't mean to be loud." His friend's head was bowed at a phone, index finger swiping up in the unmistakable toss of a fellow Trainer.

"No, it's all right," I said. "I thought you were yelling at me and I was like, how did he know I'm playing Pokémon?"

He laughed and, after a few minutes, walked over. "So, what're you working on?"

"A travel guide . . . No, I'm from Philly, but I'm on my way to New Zealand . . . To travel for a year . . . I've always wanted to do it, now was just a good time . . . Oh, that would be nice, but I have to get up early to catch my flight . . . I probably won't fly back through LA . . . Okay, well, sure, thanks."

After he left, I threw his phone number in the trash.[2]

At 7:00 a.m. the next morning, I left Los Angeles. I did not cry on the six-hour flight to Honolulu. I also did not cry in Honolulu,

---

[2] Side effects of *leaving* may include men deciding to *just go for it*. Studies show they do this because of the abysmal timing, not in spite of it. Please consult your horoscope if these symptoms persist.

where the airport had an outdoor area for reading beneath trees and calling your mom. Admittedly, I did cry on the way to Auckland. It turns out that spending two nights in LA does not break up the feeling that you're leaving. Rather, it elongates it, like a black hole is sucking you in and stretching you thinner and thinner.

After the ten-hour flight, landing in Auckland did not bring instant relief. Everyone had to remain seated so that officials could board the plane to spray our luggage and shoes with insecticide. At least, I think that's what the pilot said, as I was stretched near my limit at this point and not really listening. In any case, the spraying ritual itself—picture two figures walking up the plane aisles with raised arms misting the overhead luggage via aerosol cans, then making an about-face to do it again with lowered arms aiming for our feet—was all very serious and thus extremely amusing in my frazzled, dreamlike state.

When I was at last free of the plane, customs stood between me and the exit. Now, I don't remember where I heard this next bit of information, if it was something lingering in my head from prior research or from a friend who had traveled in Australia, but I had heard that customs in this corner of the world sometimes inspected the outdoor gear you brought with you. Chiefly, they didn't want you tracking in foreign soil that could contain foreign seeds that would spawn foreign plants. Given the insecticide incident and my haywire brain, I assumed that checking off the little box on my arrival card that said, no, I was not carrying any plants or animals with me, would not be sufficient. Taking this vague knowledge to heart, I detoured to a bathroom to scrub off my hiking boots, veterans of the Appalachians and Iceland and carrying who knows what that could singlehandedly dismantle New Zealand's ecosystem. This task involved water, very cheap toilet paper (there were no paper towels), and hopping into a stall when someone else came in. But I emerged with clean boots and the comforting knowledge that I was nearly there.

Fifteen minutes later (my boots given no more than a glance from the officials), I walked through the automatic doors of the airport and felt myself take the first steps to becoming whole again. As I departed the world of planes, airports, and stopovers, my brain slowly brought New Zealand into focus. It was close to midnight. Warm air enveloped but did not stifle me. Auckland's city center, when I deboarded the airport shuttle, was quiet and covered by the veil of night.

What would I see when the sun came up? Now that I had finally left, who would I be?

Beyond the Mountains

Mahalia Solages

WE WERE THE NEIGHBORHOOD KING POLE. WE WERE THE EYE, SOCIAL MECCA, and garden apothecary. The two-room home my husband built me sat on our large yard. We had piglets snuffing about for scraps, a donkey, a mutt, slick goats, and chickens that occasionally swaggered through my bitter cerasee and herbs, despite the spirals of the barbed wire. The valley air was sweetened by the smoldering cane, along with the scent of tobacco embedded in the pelts of bleary mules dragging behind peddlers.

We hardly befriended whichever missionary lived across from us. We simply observed, squatting on our porch, mumbling criticisms while mindlessly peeling mangoes with our teeth.

Over the years, waves of missionary groups inhabited a ten-acre property in Thomonde, Haiti, that spread back to the mountain base. Most seeking a reprieve—as many wanted and unwanted do, settling in nondescript towns in third world countries. The villagers offered the missionary skeptical smiles as they trod the footpath that arced around his property to the river. But my husband said this one, Pastor Robert, was not only planning an orphanage but a church and clinic as well.

WHEN THE MISSIONARY NEEDED help, my husband excavated the well and repaired the roof over the decrepit, corrugated metal shed the missionary called Little Angels Orphanage.

My husband's shirts were crisping in the sun as they dressed a skeletal shrub when the missionary walked over. He had two wooden chairs—one big, one small, both missing seats and needing re-caning.

My husband was raking the yard with dried coconut inflorescence, and I was preparing lunch.

"For you." He extended the chairs to my husband. The shifty-eyed missionary then pointed to my herb bundles drying on the porch. Foreigners always spoke too loud, emphasized syllables too much, and used too many words. In his choppy Creole, he said, "What are those plant things that you have sitting there today?"

I crossed my arms and crunched on day-old burnt rice from my cupped hand. "Remedies." I shifted on my haunches, moved toward my firepit, and adjusted my pot on the charcoal. I lifted the lid and stirred the cornmeal that didn't require disturbance.

Another time we sold him leaves for his ailments. Did I have something for his cold? *Hibiscus*. How about a stomachache? *Cerasee*. Did I have anything because he was hot? *Lettuce tisane*. How about sleeping? *How long do you want to sleep?* Whispering mosquitoes? *Eucalyptus and lemongrass smudge.*

One day he gave us a can of cerulean blue paint. Pastor Robert walked away with a jerking, resistant chicken in his armpit and clutching a handful of my homemade coconut brittle as our thanks.

We stroked color over our cinder block home, speaking in proverbs.

My husband looked at me. "We're eating with the devil; hold our spoons at arms' length."

"That thing you're smelling is already roasting in my fire."

THE PASTOR'S PASTIME WAS looking up at the stars and boiling water. Daily we would see him pulling up the bucket and hear it scrape along the cinder block edge when it reached the top of the well. He tied a knotted rope to trees and strung a makeshift shower stall made with sheets.

Whenever we saw the blister crossing the road heading our way, we ordered our three-year-old son inside.

In this village, we called each other brother and sister, hugged and kissed without being related. In the evenings, we would see the missionary craning his neck to catch glimpses of our activity. Oil sizzled with appetizers, boys knocked marbles, and at the domino table, heated discussions intertwined with laughter, like the braids we styled. I also performed herbal baths and remedies.

He would slink by as we ladled Sunday butternut squash soup in mugs and bowls. We watched him nibble at the beef chunks, taste the cannelloni, cabbage, and carrots. With the back of his spoon, he pushed the root vegetables before holding his breath to circle the malanga and name in his mouth.

We didn't know where he got the boys for the orphanage. He had gone farther than the surrounding towns. The boys were constantly running errands that they delivered to the pastor's hut. He had one disabled preteen named Jean, with dull chalky brown skin as if there were still remnants of flour in the sack he thread his spindly deformities through.

Pastor Robert was always at Saturday market day by the river. On market day, the villagers sold items such as secondhand clothes, brittle, alimentary items, and toiletries. Rice was measured in soup tins; potatoes were weighed in rusty Greenland milk cans, and citrus fruit was sold in piles. We spent a great deal of time observing, working through stalks of sugarcane, and spitting pulp into our fists. He would come upon us with his prowling gait, trying to barter. Even stray dogs sidestepped in a wide arc as if avoiding his exploration of hunger.

When he said, "Did you see that little boy carry that little girl across the river? She had a huge bundle on her back. The boys are so strong and masculine at that age. Such unctuous skin. So gallant." That's when LaMercy sold him the pile of large grapefruit we knew consisted of all thick rind. We then offered to cook for the orphanage to throw an eye, as we say.

When we squatted at the river's edge to hand-wash our clothes, waves of murky, soapy water gliding down the bank gave rhythm to cocooned convictions, judgment, and suspicions.

The missionary would meander, rinsing his feet. Sometimes it was the way his hands would drool over the kids' shoulders while he balanced to put his sandals back on, as if his hands were thirsty, just as the river water salivated over the boulders. It was the way he crouched by the stepping-stones at the narrowing of the river to watch the children—as if he wanted to eat them. He would walk along with the shrubbery until he perched on the tree with the protruding root high like a curved knuckle. He had a protracted gawk, sometimes closing his eyes inhaling their earthiness as if they were ripe mangoes.

MY HUSBAND AND I were sharing a pipe on our porch and eating. I was scraping oily, scorched rice from a pot, passing him crunchy spoonfuls. We watched shadows moving across the way. I got up to do the dishes.

"He found a couple of teen orphan boys to help build the playground," my husband said. "He found two girls as well."

My fingers dug into the soapy steel wool as I rotated the pot. "Syrup draws the ants."

The shaggy slouch appeared before us.

"Oh, Nelda, I think it's going to rain tonight; I could feel it." He slithered above me, wringing his hands. "My generator, no gas. There will be a lot of no-good mosquitoes. Do you have the lemongrass tisane to help me sleep and something for my arthritis, please?"

I kept scrubbing, focusing on the pot. Did this peculiar man come here to heal himself? He said he studied plants in school and wanted my help with herbal remedies for the clinic. What medicine was the clinic going to give?

"Ginger, aloe, and turmeric are good for arthritis." I slapped my foamy hands on my apron. Soapy clusters dotted the ground. "It won't rain tonight, but I'll make you something."

"Thank you." He looked at the pots and dishes. "Did you save any banana porridge for your son?"

"Yes, I take care of my own."

"I'll send Jean. He can bring it to me."

I looked at him. "I'll bring the tea."

I hunted through my garden. Under the reaper pepperbush, I tore at the thick bed of flowers, mimosa, and paracress—an anesthetic and relaxant. Stepping along the lemongrass, I found clove. In the far corner, lime flower. I knew I had gall bile from the piglet we had roasted.

"Beyond the mountains are more mountains," my husband said.

"I know." I rapidly drummed all the plants in my mortar and pestle. I scooped the paste into a pot of boiling water.

"We can teach them how to play dominoes, use a machete, and cook," my husband said.

"Misfortune doesn't have a horn." I stirred in the pig bile. "Tomorrow, I'll make them soursop tea—for shock."

My husband nodded.

I added sugar and crushed lemon. I brought the missionary the cup of tea. He wished me good night. I went home.

There wasn't a shrill, or howl, nor crickets. I didn't wake up to the smell of smoke that night. I knew the missionary would remain fused to his bed, licked in flames. There was only a crackling bloom rising, misting the moon.

Gretel's Revenge

Sue Storts

Brother, Hansel, tattled on me,
pulled my hair and hit me.
When the grown-ups weren't around
he stomped my feet and bit me.

Our mother never witnessed this,
his innocence pretended.
She'd pat his head and then blame me.
No malice he intended.

Life was Hell with such a bully,
felt his torment every day.
Hansel teased and poked and jeered.
I plotted ways to make him pay.

On our way to school one day
we saw a childhood's dream.
A mansion made of gingerbread,
bonbons, and chocolate cream.

"Why'd she put candy on her house
if not for kids to eat it?"
As we approached, an angry voice said,
"Scram, you kids! Now, beat it!"

I said, "We'll get in trouble."
Hansel ate a piece of door.
He stuck it in his mouth and then
he smiled and grabbed some more.

A plump old woman just inside
cried, "Please don't eat my house."
My brother burst his way inside.
I entered like a mouse.

"Give us all your sweets, old witch.
We're tired of your bitchin'."
"Of course." The woman smiled at us
and led us to her kitchen.

"The cookies should be ready soon.
Come see. They're almost done."
She opened the huge oven door.
"Bad children can have none."

Hansel pushed her to the floor,
leaned far inside to see.
My leg had quite a spasm, kicked
his backside with my knee.

I slammed shut the oven door,
astonished by my act.
The kindly woman's eyes met mine.
We formed a kind of pact.

She offered me a plate of cake
to help assuage my fear.
"Young men can be so clumsy.
Have a gingerbread man, my dear."

Resurrection Mary

Kipling Knox

IN FREEZING RAIN, A PICKUP SLIDES TO A STOP WHERE I STAND READY FOR this night's promise. The wind comes horizontally, painting white ice on fields, roads, fenceposts. Dark spirits, sensing vulnerability on such a night, rush in chaotic flocks over the land, chattering and obscuring. Before the pickup window opens, I appear in full view, framed by the door and hazy in the wet glass, my smile cheery as a daisy in winter. Two young men sit in the front seat, blowing warmth into their hands. These two I chose when I saw the headlights up the highway. But I am surprised to see there is a another one, in the back, an old man. He thrusts his fists into his jacket and keeps his eyes forward, like a child accused of cheating. I am unprepared for three.

The driver says, Where's your car? His name is Caleb.

I have no car, I reply. Usually it's fine to walk here.

Jeffrey, the passenger, says, You must have walked a long way. Nothing around.

I look up the road, squinting, contemplating. The longer I hold this moment, the deeper I set the hook. But should I? I've attempted three only once, and failed. I look back and see Jeffrey study me—not my body but my face. The fear is heavy in his eyes and on his breath. It manifests as sadness, resignation, but beneath that he is terrified. Like black water rushing beneath pack ice. I have to try.

I say, Storm just came out of nowhere.

Well, says Caleb, do you need a ride?

I look at him and hold it. He is inscrutable, the fierce face of an owl feeding chicks, but delicately. I look at Jeffrey, whose eyes water in the cold, whose mouth is soft.

Would you mind? I ask.

Course not, Caleb says. Get in.

I turn to the rear door, but the old man doesn't budge. Neither does he move his head but I hear him say, Leave three hours late, now you want to pick up stray women. This rate I'll be dead before Wisconsin.

Jeffrey says, I can scooch over. And so he does, straddling the drive shaft lump underfoot. The truck is just as cold inside. The hole for a radio is stuffed with rags. The cab must reek with the odors of mildew, petroleum, and men. But I am spared of this sense.

I arrange myself on the seat, taking half a man's width, and hold my hat in my lap. Jeffrey excuses himself, reaches across me, pulls the truck door shut.

All set? Caleb asks.

The old man strikes the back of the seat and says, For Christ's sake, drive! We want to make Montaner by morning it ain't gonna happen pickin' up whores roadside.

Caleb works the shifter until the truck catches a gear. The tires spin and the tail drifts out as we take to the road. He looks at me around Jeffrey's solemn profile. Here comes the unavoidable question.

Where you heading?

I could wince. How many times have these three words spilled out on a highway in America? A tryptic of words that bear all the images of possibility, promise, tragedy. For ten generations, the phrase endures without improvement, whose tired formula signifies for so many a pivot in their course of events, whose simple question marks the interminable movement and collision of people across this continent, helping and hurting, saving and killing, inspiring a thousand dreadful stories of a folklore drawn down by its coarseness, its banality, its weak chicory facsimile of the European masters. It's a sorry phrase, but it's our phrase, and I seek it every night.

Just to the cemetery, I say. And so we are off.

UNDER PRESSURE OF THE wind, the truck begins to drift across the shoulder line, and Caleb corrects it. He says, What cemetery? Nothing for the next fifty miles but corn and Casey's.

You'll see it when I show you, I say. It's easy to miss. I can walk from there.

How far?

Not far.

I could just drive you home—it's no problem.

The old man interjects, Take the lady where she wants, all right?

Caleb lets out a breath and adjusts his rearview mirror. Jeffrey balls his fist and bounces it on Caleb's knee, just once.

Are you traveling far? I ask. Are you from around here?

Jeffrey says, We're going to Idaho. He hovers his hand over his mouth when he talks, surely because he feels we are too close.

Driving straight through? I ask.

Naw, stopping in Montana. He adds, If this storm don't blow us off the road.

And you started where?

Middling County, basically, Caleb says. Not far back. But it was a heck of a lot warmer down there, I'll tell you what.

They laugh together awkwardly—although it wasn't quite a joke, it was good enough.

I nod. And now it's time for me to be quiet, and let silence fall over the cab, let their minds begin to work until their energies betray them and I grow familiar with their particular instance of fear. All of it will come. It feels heavy and oppressive, like a cold fog in a river bottom. Each man has been nurturing this fear, what they feel necessary for survival, since their memories began. They are artisans of the material, turning fear into rage, bitterness, hatred, contempt. It destroys their perception and deprives them of tranquility. A person at peace would have mentioned my dance-hall dress, my impractical pearly shoes, my rakish bonnet unaffected by sleet. But they see none of it, so bright are their fantasies. We sit in silence and hear the tires howl and the windshield wipers snap and the tailpipe rumble. They clear their throats. From the back seat the old man snuffs his nose repeatedly, a bloodhound blasting a scent.

ORDINARILY IT'S JUST ONE man. Take last night. A bald, bearded man somewhere in the disoriented middle of his life drove home towing a boat. His vast vehicle, black as a water moccasin, swallowed up his small form. So much car for so little man.

I could use some company, he said, and cleared lunch wrappers from the passenger seat. He expressed surprise at how easily I climbed into the car.

I told him I was lonely too, to measure his excitement and vulnerability. He dropped his guard and began explaining how badly his wife disrespected him, for his priorities, his taste in entertainment, his political views.

He confessed, We both knew it was a consolation prize when she married me. The other boyfriend, her so-called great love, got religion one day and said she wasn't good enough. So she gets me. I guess I made it worse 'cause of all that. Anyway. She hates my dad because one Christmas she made him a sweater and he put it on his beagle. But it's my job to hate that old bastard, not hers.

He turned and smiled at me, whitened teeth behind whiskers. Not sure why I'm telling you this, he said. After a moment's reflection, he added. She's pretty though, I'll grant her that. Even now, after everything.

Then he looked at me, one wrist draped over the wheel, and said, Not as pretty as you, though.

I told him I thought we could talk more easily if he pulled over. He glanced at me with eagerness, his thumbs tapping the steering wheel. He guided the giant vehicle to the shoulder with intense concern for his boat, craning his neck and checking mirrors. But once he parked, he dropped out of his door without a word and came around the truck. By the time he reached my door, he was readying parts of his clothing—buttons, zippers, all the gates that restrain our wild impulses. And when I said no I really just wanted to talk, to just sit still together along the road for a while, he said he knew better, he knew that game, and he came for me through the open door. He missed the running board with his small western boot and stumbled. He glared as if it were my doing. Now his fear had grown to a lopsided mushroom larger than himself—fear of embarrassment, of public shame, of the cruel voice that condemns him with almost every thought. And the fear transformed to aggression and he made a little hop up to the cab and lunged for me.

When he seized nothing, when his stout arms collapsed on themselves, the aggression melted and there was nothing but unadulterated fear. A boy who's seen a ghost. Now I could commence my promise.

IT ALL HAPPENS IN less than a second.

First, the scene of my demise unfolds before me, and at the moment of impact it blackens, and my awareness shifts to the heavens and I breathe deeply. I reach in all directions, past the moon, planets, farther out into nebula where stars are born, into undulating mesh of dark matter—I open myself to all this energy and let it fill me up from the balls of my feet to the crown of my head. And then, empowered by such a charge, I pounce on the man.

He feels nothing but the impact of the energy—no flesh or nails or hot breath—just the overwhelming force flattening him backward and crushing him against the road bed. I fly at him like a great cat, long-fanged and muscular, and thrust my fierce face into his, spreading his flesh so his eyes stick open and dry and he has to witness my fury and determination. His face thus open and his spine flattened and his skull shocked, he becomes as tender as an orchid petal. Holding my terrible gaze, filling his field of vision, I sap his amygdala until it ceases to function. I seize the hippocampus into a trembling suspension. I flush the man of adrenocorticotropic hormone and epinephrine and norepinephrine and corticotropin releasing factor. He becomes, in moments, physiologically incapable of fear.

Then I release him, my remaining fury dissipating into the night. He rolls to his side and hugs his knees to his chest and begins to sob, gently.

I STOOD WITH MY arms crossed and my chin lowered, smiling like a sister. There's no need to be sad, I told the small man. I extended my arm and hand as you would to help someone up. But just far enough he couldn't reach it.

The man sat up, elbows on knees, eyes looking beyond the road with an expression of simple wonder.

I don't know why, he said. He wiped his cheeks with flat palms and said, I don't know why. This never happens.

Through his eyes, now, emerged his four-year-old self. The self who nursed a wounded toad in a box beneath his bed until his father found it. The one who searched for his lost classmate in a straw maze in the barn and hugged her when she was found. Who cried when he saw his grandfather's shelf of medicine. Who escorted a caterpillar from the street to a milkweed in a school lot where older boys chased him down like a rodeo calf.

Temporarily depleted of his anger reserves, drained of the fear he had cultivated since the sap rose in him—now he could listen and receive.

Why are you wearing that dress? He asked. You look so old-fashioned.

I came from a dance, I said. Thank you for asking.

Did you enjoy the dance? Do you like dancing? Were you with a boyfriend? His questions came urgently, earnestly.

I did. I do. I was with my husband. We are both gone now.

His face fell into concern, but before he could ask more questions, I said, I want to show you something.

I led him down a tractor road along a drainage ditch and up a gradual slope until we could see the horizon curving in the arc of the planet. Lights dotted the night—distant grain elevators, wind turbines, cell towers, urban glow from crossroad towns.

Just wait, I said. We're patient.

The man stood with arms hanging loosely, shoulders curved, chin up.

Car tires cried shrill on the highway, the lights of industry glowed, a breeze carried agricultural dust.

But then, all that faded, and the phantoms of the lost prairie emerged. First a flock of a thousand pigeons, feathers of light in gold and blue, rushed overhead. A ghostly avian aurora. A herd of tiny deer, whose translucent legs glowed fine as silk strands, bounded from the ditch. A troop of purple hairy men came just after and chased them with ancient weapons. A wagon train of prairie schooners rumbled from beyond the horizon toward us, steel-wrapped wheels sparking against the stones of the field, the driver a pink smear of light, drooping in exhaustion, barely able to lift his whip against the draft horse, whose eyes glowed white and rolled back like enormous eggs. And along the distant ridge, in silhouette from an unseen glow, marched a line of mastodon. They might have been cut of art paper, but they shone deep blue, like ocean water at dusk, a blue so dark it only appears against black. One mastodon lifted her trunk, rolled back her head, and bellowed a note of doleful horns. The last of the herd, a small one whose curling tusks outsized his head, stumbled, fell back from his position, then ran to catch the others, and then they all disappeared beyond the horizon, disinterested in what happened here.

In moments we saw specters from all ages, walking in solemn luminescence across the molested land. But it was no mourning. Only witness to existence, the evidence of everything. I explained things to the man. He listened, asked few questions. His gaze drew down to the ground, unfocused. I fulfilled my promise, as best I could.

Dark spirits came then, as magpies to a carcass, chattering and circling, sensing the man's vulnerability. I swatted at them, shooed them. They formed a bunch between us and the man's vehicle, obscuring it, erasing light. I flew at them and they scattered.

I stood by the roadside and waved as the man left. He used his turn signal and accelerated up the road delicately. He returned my wave and was gone. Then the mustard seed of fear began to take hold again in his acid belly, and I will never know if he gained what he needs to control it. But we made the effort. We resisted the inexhaustible descent.

THESE THREE MEN—CALEB, Jeffrey, and the old man—they won't be so easy. They are comfortable riding in silence. By now most men would have started conversation. Some men joke, some confess, some flirt, everyone talks, eventually. But not these three. They sit like prisoners, wholly preoccupied. This impermeability makes them so much more difficult. And there are three.

Caleb points to the glove box. Jeffrey gives me a polite glance and reaches over, taking a pack of cigarettes. He lights two and gives one to Caleb. He passes the pack back to the old man, who grunts his acceptance. We continue riding.

IN EARLIER DAYS, WHEN I felt my most capable, when legends of my practice had spread among the living and the dead and I believed the stories they told, on a humid summer's night, I attempted this many. Three MBA students in a German sedan drove home after a wild night in the city. They saw me in their headlights almost too late and slammed the car into a slide, then reversed wildly and greeted me through open windows.

I thought they would be simple. The one in the back seat feared he would never be loved. The front passenger feared the others would recognize him as an imposter to their elite caste. And the driver feared the disdain of his parents, where even a scratch on that car would represent his hopelessness. They were polite at first, giddy, speaking in a slang of their invention. But inevitably the one in the back reached out to try the seam of my dress and found nothing there. He began to scream, What the fuck are you? and the driver pulled violently off the road.

Even then, I didn't give up on my promise. I had never endured failure. I beckoned them out of the car and only the front passenger came, to prove himself to the other two. His fear of me was overripe and reeking, but his terror of embarrassment was stronger. Encouraged by his vulnerability, I flew at him. But he was athletic and turned in time to avoid the rush. My advance hit the car and I imprinted hand marks on the door frame—deep impressions in the steel that would later appear in testimonials of my legend, identical to those in the gate of the cemetery.

I managed to get to the athletic man, and I reduced him to his boyhood and made him wait—just for two seconds, I said, while we got the others.

Sometimes the burst of energy manifests as light, a pop and flash visible for miles, and the phantoms of night pause and look toward me. In those days I savored their attention. People are the most interested and amazed. The common animals skitter wide-eyed and respectful. Something extraordinary had happened in the fabric of space, in the membrane between corporeal and ethereal. It fueled the legend. Only the most ancient creatures ignored these events of my concoction. The mastodon cared least of all.

Such a blast of light came from inside the sedan as I rushed at the driver, whom I considered the most difficult of the three. But he also ducked in time—not a reaction to my move, which isn't possible, but rather a premeditated act in motion when I pounced. And so I glanced off this man, knocking some of his senses askew, but not all of them. As I repositioned, the dark spirits arrived in a dense flock, and burrowed in the vulnerable man. By the time I drove them away, he was sick.

I finally admitted failure, and didn't attempt the backseat man who had originally groped me. He was screaming, pressing himself down into the crease of the seat, as if he might push himself into the safety of the trunk. His face was distorted, his eyes pathetic—now, another kind of child, but one of absolute terror rather than compassion. I had broken the fundamental tenet of my promise, leaving more suffering in the world, not less. All three were compromised in their own way. I retreated and drifted around the fields aimlessly for nights, until my resolve returned.

By the time they reached their home downstate, the boys had recovered and invented a story that would make my legend vulgar. I had been their willing servant, and they had completed their rite of conquest. How many friends and sons will they infect with this fable? It's possible that I'm still making up for this cruel math, in every promise that follows that night.

So WHAT MAKES ME think I can manage these three men after such a failure? Every point of reason suggests I should leave them immediately, spring that rattling door open and drop into the night like a scarf in the wind. But I can't give it up, yet. It would be another wasted night and although the debt of life can never be repaid, I believe it can be reduced. This keeps me in the seat. I think, Perhaps if I try to understand . . .

What are your plans in Idaho? I ask.

Caleb grips the wheel with both hands and says, We have a duty, ma'am.

Call me Mary, I say. What duty?

Patriotic duty, ma'am, that's all. We have a situation at the border. Infidels.

The old man erupts from behind, Caleb can you shut your trap and turn the goddamn radio on?!

Radio's broke, Dad. Broke since we got it.

I feel the old man kick the back of the seat. What kind of man are you, Cal, can't even get a radio in your truck. And you can't keep your mouth shut, neither, telling every whore comes along our plans.

Then the old man's face is right behind my ear as he says to me in a low tone, Don't you breathe a word of this to no one, ever. You hear me, girl? Not a goddamned soul. You never seen us, never had a conversation, nothing. Or we come for you next.

Caleb glances in the rearview mirror. His voice grows tauter, fiddle strings turned tight. That's enough, Dad. Have a drink.

Jeffrey puts his hand on Caleb's thigh. Caleb pushes the hand away quickly, but leaves his on the seat. They both look ahead. I smile at them, but they won't meet my eyes.

Have a drink, the old man mutters. The kid tells me to have a drink. Like that's all I got left in this life. You have a drink, you wuss.

He snuffs outward again, bloodhound. His voice tails off, You have a goddamn drink.

I AM STILL THINKING this group may not be right for my promise tonight. I am considering leaving the cab of the truck while it blasts seventy miles per hour down an icy highway in Illinois. They will argue about what happened for the rest of their lives. But come Idaho, it will all fade in the urgency of their crusade.

But there is Caleb's hand gripping the wheel as if to wring it dry. There is Jeffrey's right knee pumping up and down like a mad oil derrick. There is the old man snuffing and snuffing and kicking, a toddler in an airplane seat. There is sickness to be healed. They feel sorry for me, that is plain, and they are not seduced. But there is a greasy smoke of fear from them that will yield no good in this world. And the bed of the truck is full of weapons, I can feel that too. It would have been easy to surmise this, but I didn't have to. So it continues.

IN THE SLEET BESIDE the road I can see phantoms. A woman in bare feet and a summer dress peers into a drainage ditch, alone. She glows light green, frets her hands against her dress, glances up at me as we pass. A family of coyote radiate in slack-limbed rust-colored form, heads below their shoulders, all in a file trotting the highway just as we pass through them. Another woman hangs over the guardrail of a bridge, her body bent as a sapling—legs in the road, head hanging over the side like squash on a vine. A man comes on all fours up the embankment onto the shoulder, dragging a limp child. He and the child glow orange—their faces follow as the truck passes. A translucent whitetail deer bolts just beyond the weak headlights and runs, springing from yellow line to line, then vanishes in the dark. A family of long-legged raccoon, now just light in the dark red of pomegranate, swim through the young corn where in life they gorged themselves.

The men beside me see none of this. I don't know why. I never saw it either. I search for the mastodon, for the bison, the older beasts. They are not here tonight.

JEFFREY LOOKS AT ME, smiles, then looks away. Hand over mouth he says, I love that vintage dress. If you don't mind my saying. Must be cold though. You lose your coat?

Thank you, I say. You notice things.

He waits for me to answer and he gets no satisfaction.

You're married? he asks, pointing to my ring finger.

I was, I say.

Oh, I'm so sorry.

Caleb glances and clears his throat. He shakes his head as condolence.

The sleet turns to heavy rain, overwhelming the wipers. Caleb slows the truck.

Can I ask, Jeffrey says, what happened? If you don't mind my asking?

I tell them the truth. They won't remember it anyway, so long as I fulfill the promise.

We were in Chicago. A night like this, actually, and the sleet made a rind on the rooftops, the cars, the railroad tracks, umbrellas. The whole city sparkled, white lights on icing. We were out dancing. We were always out dancing. The only time we didn't fight was when we danced, and then we were perfect—two vines as one trunk, swans in a lagoon, hands in prayer. We barely spoke but only danced and drank until the club thinned out. Word spread that travel was dangerous. I wanted to stay. He wanted to go. He called me a drunk; I called him a monster. We glared at each other and danced another number. Finally, I agreed to go. I had my shoes in my hand, like I do now.

My gosh, you do, says Jeffrey. I totally missed that.

Me too, says Caleb, with a whiff of unease.

I continue.

It was easier to walk on the ice in my bare feet. I felt nothing. I slid and danced. My husband barked at me. He tried to catch me but slid on the sidewalk and fell hard on his side. As he pulled himself up, he slid and fell again. I laughed. Eventually we got in the car. He was furious with me. He called me a tart. I called him a coward. I felt the back of his hand crash my mouth, tasted blood, but felt no pain. I hit back, a fist to the fleshy ear. He kept bringing the back of his hand, weighted with class ring. The car slid and drifted on the icy pavement. With the sudden loss of traction came a disorientation I had never felt—a nauseating, total loss of control. Cars honked as we drifted in our ton of metal and glass. People called warnings. I cursed him until I didn't know what I was saying—brutal, hurtful words that erupted straight from my gut. He reached over me, driving his shoulder into my head, unlatched my door, and pushed me out. I tumbled into the street, sliding on my dress, felt the wet cold and the asphalt pebbles on my hands and thighs. My fate, my destiny, my actions were not my own. I belonged to the night, the weather, the careening cars in a horrific dance in an ice-clad city.

I pause my story, waiting for one of them to draw a breath—the sign that someone is about to say something. None of them does. The old man snuffs, but I can feel his attention. I continue.

While I tumbled down the street, followed by my husband, another car raced toward us. It was one of those new, enormous sedans, with bench seats you could sleep on. From where I slid, splayed like a lizard, head up observing—I saw three people in the front seat. A man and two children. So plain in the streetlights, in all the glamorous reflection of the avenue. The man's face was compressed in anger. But the children just stared without judgment. A boy and a girl, chins just above the dashboard, looked out at this lady in a dress in the street, at this reckless man swerving a car with side door flapping. The boy, the girl, whose faces were painted with wonder, seemed to ask, Is this something that happens? My sight grew shockingly keen. I could see the wet of the girl's lip around a crooked lower tooth. The boy's delicate nostrils flared. Their eye color was identical, a golden-brown around dilated pupils. The steering wheel was enormous, thin, light blue, crenellated. A toy elephant stood on the dash, unprepared for the crash.

Then I lost their faces behind the great chrome bumper and the car bounced over me and demolished my husband's car such that the motor rammed through his ribcage.

I END THE STORY, just short of the moment I made my promise to those children.

We listen to the highway noises for a while. I wear a thousand-yard stare, as if in a trance. I await their reactions, to see if it helps me understand.

Jeffrey says, So you were . . . you're okay now?

Oh yes, I say. I'm fine.

The old man says, You should've listened to him. Should've gotten the fuck out of that club when he said so.

Jeffrey says, That's not fair. It's not like he's the boss of her.

Caleb whispers, Dude.

The old man strikes, quick as a snake. He stiff-arms the back of Jeffrey's head with his flat palm. In that instant, I see his fingernails, wooden and yellow.

Just as quickly, Caleb whips his right arm around the back of the seat, swatting at his father, but makes no contact.

The old man seethes, No fairy's gonna backtalk me. You keep your opinions to yourself. Better yet, you get yourself some proper opinions. Afore they eat you up in Idaho. I may be dead by then so I won't be able to provide protection and Caleb ain't worth a shit—

Caleb yells, Shut the fuck up! Just shut up! Right? You fucking hear me?

The old man flicks Caleb in the parietal bone—a practiced flick that makes a sharp rap. Caleb swings back again, the truck swerves across the center line, and his hand glances over Jeffrey's forehead on its way.

Oh, I'm sorry, Caleb says. His face is suddenly compassionate. Then he lectures, Dad if you don't behave yourself I swear I'll turn this truck around and cancel the whole mission. I'll do it. Seriously, I will.

I HAVE NO BUSINESS taking on these three. If I think I can control this situation, I have learned nothing these many years. They aren't worth it. Then again, if I could fulfill the promise with these men, how much suffering might I prevent? It could be my greatest night, could reverse the damage I've caused. But no, it's no good, this situation.

I say, Can we pull over? You can drop me off here. It's fine: I can walk.

Caleb studies me. I can see he's about to argue, to point out rational objections. But he refrains. He says, Sure. Just let me find a spot.

The old man shouts from the back seat, No one's stopping this truck! You think I got time to kill? We let her out next filling station. That's what.

Caleb sighs. That doesn't make sense, Dad. We didn't give her a ride to just take her to some random gas station.

Then Caleb says to me, quietly, Don't worry.

Jeffrey raises his hand, almost drops it to my knee in reassurance, but stops just short.

The old man continues yelling, Who you telling not to worry? Some goddamn tramp you don't even know? How about my worry? Sitting in the back of this truck worrying about one last chance I get to do something decent, worthwhile? For once! Just one thing before I keel over. And you messing it up over some goddamn girl. How about that worry?

Jeffrey turns in his seat to give the old man a look of understanding, of calm. Look, he says, it's gonna be all right. We'll just pull over quick and drop her off and then we'll be on our way. It's the right thing to do.

The old man spits his reply, punctuating each word, Who. Are. You to tell me what's all right or what's not? You prancing through life like a girl with a pecker putting notions in people's heads, notions in my son's head? I've told you before and I'm not warning you again to not backtalk me. You shut up. You follow orders.

Caleb shouts, a sudden eruption, Nobody asked you, Dad! Nobody fucking asked you!

The old man punches Caleb's headrest. I don't need permission. When I say we don't stop, we don't stop.

Guys, Jeffrey pleads. Can we just—

Don't bother, Caleb says.

No, says Jeffrey, listen, guys. We're going to make it to Idaho just fine. Emotions are just running high. Everybody take a deep breath.

The old man is silent now, but I can feel his raging anxiety. He is overwhelmed with it, speechless. Perhaps I should take him on right now, in the moving truck. I could subdue him in two seconds, probably. But that could be too much for Caleb. It could cause a crash. I just need to get out of the truck and let this one go.

Could you crack the window? I ask Jeffrey. Just give me a hand with this crank?

Sure, says Jeffrey, and he begins to move.

But suddenly the old man punches and kicks Caleb's seat, a tantrum. Keep that goddamned window closed! Freezing enough in here! This girl's got some spell over you two fairies and it's about to ruin our mission, you doing everything she says.

I begin to consider again taking the old man on now. But I want to calm the situation, bring some net of control over it.

We don't have to pull over, I say.

That's right, listen to the fucking whore! The old man screams. She knows who's the goddamn boss around here. Thank you, you fucking whore.

That's too much. I turn to face him over the seat.

He stares back, bewildered, furious. What the fuck are you looking at?!

Caleb reaches out a hand toward me. It's gentle but I retreat instinctively. He withdraws his hand and says, Sorry.

Jeffrey puts a hand on Caleb's shoulder and says, Just keep your eyes on the road, buddy. Just drive.

I SEE THE OLD, twisted car bumper on the road as we speed toward it. Caleb does not.

Dark spirits have gathered outside, flying across the road like torn shingles in the wind, as if they sense something is going wrong here. They obscure Caleb's vision, though he doesn't know it. To him it's just one of those strangely black nights.

The line of the wheel draws over the bumper precisely, and the explosion of the tire jolts all of their hearts into racing.

Caleb grips the wheel against the sudden pull of the truck. We're fine, we're fine, he says. Just a flat. Goddamn old bumper—I didn't see it.

He slows the truck and searches for a wide spot on the shoulder.

The old man lets out a sob and drops his face in his hands.

How could you not see that, you dumb shit? he cries. You can't even drive right, for fuck's sake. Now how much time are we gonna lose fixing this wheel? If it can even be fixed? All this because you pick up some girl and get distracted? You dumb shit. You dumb, fucking shit . . . I might as well die now, with not a goddamn thing to show but a dumb shit son doesn't know how to drive.

He moans, his head still down.

With remarkable speed, Caleb retrieves the jack and puts it in place. The rest of us are out of the truck now. Jeffrey crouches to help. The old man puts his fists in his jeans pockets and thrusts his face toward the scene, his cap low over his brow. I prepare to leave, considering what I'll tell them that might be plausible but so subtle it vanishes from their memories soon.

The old man says, It's gonna fall, you set it up like that.

Caleb is under the truck now, looking for damage to the axle. He looks up at his ranting father. Would you just shut up for a minute? Seriously, can I just fix this without you going on like a fucking idiot?

The old man kicks the fender and the truck sways uneasily on its jack.

I want to get away from this man. He is unsalvageable. He just needs to die, preferably somewhere far from others, where his hot energy will decay toxically, like spent uranium. When this man dies, no one will want to be near what manifests.

But I see Jeffrey stabilize the truck, offer encouraging words to Caleb, who takes short breaths, straining to pull off the wheel. The tire is a shredded bloom of rubber. A black peony.

The old man stiff-arms the truck with both hands. The truck sways again, dangerously.

Jesus! Jeffrey yells. Fucking stop it, dude!

The old man takes a long step toward Jeffrey and puts his face close. Don't you fucking call me dude. Call me sir, or better yet, don't say nothing.

Jeffrey looks him back in the eyes and laughs. You sad, little man, he says.

Without warning, the old man jerks up his knee and rams it between Jeffrey's thighs. Jeffrey folds forward and drops.

CALEB IS UP ON his feet now rushing toward his father. He grabs the old man's shoulders and slams his back into the truck. The old man releases a bellow of air and Caleb stands back, surprised by what he's done.

I am wondering what would happen if I release my promise on them now. I am concerned but also curious. Could they survive? In all that clash of energy would I survive, or perhaps evolve into some other form?

Caleb goes to help Jeffrey. The old man drops to all fours, pulls in a wheezy breath, and then scrambles to the back of the pickup. He opens the hatch and retrieves an assault rifle. He turns to face all three of us, gun hanging from both hands, chest heaving. I am thinking, Now that gun has to go off. It's inexorable.

But Caleb moves as lithe as a ferret, and snaps the rifle away and strikes his father in the head with the butt. One, quick, well-practiced jab of the gun stock to the super orbital ridge, and the old man's skull splits like a dropped pumpkin.

He falls, dead.

I know this before the boys do. They are on their knees trying to revive him. They are both sobbing, not for the old man but for the shock of the moment. All the rest of their lives will be defined by this one act, and every decision made thereafter will cascade from Caleb's act and they both know it. There are no reactions equal to this event, so they do the best humans can do and cry. They shake the old man. Caleb attempts CPR but only manages to crack a rib.

For a minute they sit back on their knees and pant, looking at the man. Then they turn and look at me.

JEFFREY PUTS HIS ARMS around Caleb to console him. Don't shut down on me now, he says. We'll get through. None of this matters. Only us, right?

Caleb looks at me with embarrassment.

Jeffrey continues. We can go to the border, do your duty—do it in your old man's name. Anything. Don't shut down on me, Caleb. Don't go away.

He's shivering now, his lower mandible trembling visibly. Saliva drips from Jeffrey's lower lip but he is unaware. He stares at the other man.

Caleb is weak, leaning to one side, his gaze swaying like a willow branch, to one side and then the other, without purpose.

I wonder: Have I caused this? If I hadn't chosen their truck this dark night. If I hadn't entertained the possibility I could manage three this time. If I hadn't turned around and looked at the old man. If I hadn't made the promise in the instant before that boy and that girl disappeared from my sight.

Then I realize they are all watching me. Caleb looks with curiosity and perhaps a slight malevolence. I am a witness. Jeffrey considers my incongruity—my vintage dress and pearly shoes—and wonders how I came to be involved in all this. The dark spirits gather in a spiral high above—I can hear the chattering. Across the plain the phantoms emerge in shifting light, a palette of pale radiance. They lift their heads and stare. They wait to see: Will there be a flash this time?

Caleb asks, What will you do?

I have no choice.

I tilt my head back and begin the practice, filling with energy drawn down from the fabric of everything, and then I fly at the men.

It's easy and explosive. Their fear is immense and ready—as sharp as quinine, as rich as lily dew. And the blast of light comes like a thunderclap, rumbling in waves across the dark and wet fields. The specters have never seen such an emergence as this. They lower to the ground as it passes.

With placid smiles and moist eyes, Caleb and Jeffrey follow me down the steep bank to a path through a hedge, ground too depleted to plant, where wicked honeysuckle taps what nutrients remain, where dead Osage branches grasp at a dull sky.

The young men see the specters in the field now.

How are they so beautiful? Caleb asks.

Are they always there? Jeffrey asks.

Seven children made of silver light dance in a circle. A pale yellow mother lifts a baby in one arm and a cat in another and stares. Crows, black on the outside but illuminated in blue from within, flap a lazy path around us and continue west. Long-legged raccoons of multicolored light scatter up the trunks of dead trees. A farmer stands at the rise of a hill, arms down and fingers curled—he just looks away and away and away.

Then we see the mastodon. They come up over the distant rise, from where the farmer looks. They walk in a line, trunk to tail, electric blue beasts along the horizon, making their migration across the spirit of grasses and the memory of savanna. A bull rolls his head back and calls, a chorus of foghorn and brass, an exaltation of the wonder of things, and then turns toward the place where I stand. But even so, the beasts never stop marching. Their tusks nearly touch the ground and sweep up, a repeated curl, same as seashells, same as galaxies.

All phantoms, near and far, watch the mastodon pass.

When I explain it all to the young men, they barely need to hear the words. On nights when we see mastodon, my promise is easily kept. In the sight of such a thing who needs reminder of their mortality? Who needs to hear that every action prompts a reaction, continuously through time, that none of us are exempt from the balance of forces?

THEN THE YOUNG MEN, Caleb and Jeffrey, work together like classmates as I watch from the guardrail. They repair the truck. They wrap the old man's body. They struggle him into the truck bed, working his stubborn corpse, arms falling out of the shroud again and again.

They look at me and say nothing and leave with a short spin of the spare tire on gravel.

And although the old man's body speeds away down the highway, tucked in a bed of weapons, his energy remains. I feel it coalesce and rise. Soon it will gather in his form. It may be a color of light, it may be the absence of light. But very soon, he will be here. He will haunt the same highway that I rule.

He will come to know Resurrection Mary.

Bruised Ego Trip

Becky Jensen

YOU . . . ARE . . . CRUSHING IT, I THINK SMUGLY, HIKING THROUGH TALL stands of quaking aspen on the east side of Kenosha Pass.

I'm seventy miles and six days into my epic solo backpacking trip on the Colorado Trail, a 500-mile path that runs through six wilderness areas, eight mountain ranges, and six national forests between Denver and Durango. The CT is kind of like the Appalachian Trail only shorter, with more wide-open landscapes and much taller mountains. So tall, in fact, that in the five weeks it will take me to thru-hike the entire CT, I will have gained the same elevation as climbing Mount Everest, sea level to summit, three times.

For years, I have longed to do something big, some kind of wild adventure like this that would brand me as a badass. Out here, I'm responsible for no one else but me, free from kids needing dinner, clients pushing deadlines, and a boyfriend hungry to touch my imperfect body.

The trees open up to a grassy hillside sprinkled with red paintbrush flowers, and I see my first panoramic view of the snowcapped mountain ranges ahead of me. I've been walking through dense forests for so long that I had momentarily forgotten what I'm in for, namely, hundreds of miles of alpine peaks and steep trails only a few days away. I pat myself on the back for getting such good sleep the night before, and for coming so far already. Still, the landscape ahead of me is sobering.

The afternoon is a scorcher, unusually hot and bone-dry as I enter the high country. My swollen feet are starting to drag on the trail, and I stumble over a small tree root. Although I quickly recover, the misstep triggers negative self-talk, automatic and painfully familiar. *You're toeing in again, Becky. Straighten out that right foot.*

As a young child, my toes turned inward so severely they would sometimes cross and catch on one another as I walked. Dad said the best athletes, the fastest runners, were pigeon-toed like me, but Mom didn't buy it. She thought my feet were deformed, and the way I walked was a shame and needed fixing.

To this day, my pigeon-toed feet occasionally cause me to stumble. They can't be trusted in situations like this, when I'm tired and they feel like wet bags of sand as I try to walk along uneven ground. I lift each foot a little higher with every step, swinging the more troublesome right foot extra wide so it lands straight and true, so my tracks appear normal. It's always that damn right foot.

I finally emerge from the tunnel of trees. As I walk across the flat and featureless dirt parking lot, I see a woman and several children pile out of a vehicle. The kids are excited to be running around outside, and the woman, who appears to be their mother, is busy corralling them toward a sun-bleached exhibit about the South Park and Pacific Railroad. When the dust settles, I'm surprised to see an older teenage boy, maybe high school age, slowly climb out of the same car. He checks his perfectly tousled hair in the reflection of the car window, slides on a pair of sunglasses, and adjusts the collar of his jacket. The kid is working hard to look just right—in the middle of a dirt parking lot, in the middle of nowhere. I secretly name him Sunglasses.

Shaking my head, I cross the parking lot to follow a wide trail, one I assume to be the CT, which turns out to be an interpretive part of the railroad exhibit and a dead end for me. As I retrace my steps, I can see Sunglasses not far ahead, carefully walking along a single rail of the abandoned train track near the trail, arms outstretched like a tightrope walker. I catch up to him, but I am so mesmerized by his sure-footed balancing act that I have stopped paying attention to my own tired feet. The treads on my right shoe catch the top of my left shoe, and I go down hard. Nothing about my fall is slow or graceful. It is fast and cringeworthy. Rough and damaging.

I lay there motionless for a few seconds, trying to catch my breath, wondering how badly I have hurt myself. My left shoulder, hip, and knee have taken the brunt of the fall, with the full weight of my backpack adding to the force of the impact on the hardpan trail. I glance up to see Sunglasses looking at me, and then away really fast, pretending he doesn't see me and hasn't witnessed the whole embarrassing fall. He says nothing. He does nothing. I am mortified.

I could use some help, Sunglasses, I think sarcastically, but I don't ask.

My pack keeps me pinned to the ground on my left side, my free arm and leg flailing, trying to right myself like a flipped beetle. I unfasten my chest strap and hip belt, and slowly, painfully, pull my arms out of the dusty backpack, trying to keep my bloody shoulder from smearing and staining the strap. Using a trekking pole, I push myself back up, huffing and puffing, onto my feet.

Glancing up again, I lock eyes with Sunglasses, who shoots me a wide grin. "How's it going?" he asks as he balances on his imaginary tightrope.

"How's it going? Seriously?" I shriek. "Well, I don't recommend falling with a thirty-five-pound pack."

The comeback is lame, and I'm disappointed that I didn't fire off a better zinger to put this little puke in his place. No bones are broken, but my road-rash shoulder is on fire and beginning to ooze, my left hip and glute are aching, and tiny rocks are embedded under the skin of my throbbing knee. Bright red blood is running down my dusty leg and into my wool sock. I am humiliated, dirty and bleeding, feeling raw and mean.

Sunglasses grunts, gives a departing nod with his head, and walks away.

With shaking hands, I grab my heavy pack and drag it to the top of a large boulder so I can slide it onto my back. I hobble over to the gravel road that leads to the highway, hoping to pick up the CT again. Several cars kick up dust clouds, leaving me blind and coughing, as they pass. When I finally reach the highway, a wave of nausea rolls through me and I almost throw up as I stumble across the pavement.

Once I reach the other side of the road, I spy the small Kenosha Pass Campground. Public campgrounds like this often attract people who bring generators and twinkle lights, who play loud music and leave trash lying around. These campgrounds are notorious bear magnets. In my mind there is nothing badass about pitching my tent at this poor-man's KOA, but I can't take another step. I'm a bloody mess and admit with defeat that the nearby tent pad, garbage dumpster, vault toilet, and private picnic table look like a slice of heaven. *I should be tougher than this*, I think. *That's why I came out here.* But there's no getting around it; I am done for the day. Grudgingly, I shove cash into an envelope at the pay station and select a site closest to the Colorado Trail.

To my relief, there's a well with a water pump on site. I carry my first-aid kit and a clean bandana to the pump, which has a sign that says "No Bathing." I look down at my body, then up at the sign, and then down at my body again. No one is nearby, and I wash myself from head to toe, gently cleaning the angry scrapes and gashes with mild soap and water. I sit next to the pump and painstakingly pull tiny rocks out of my leg with tweezers and apply some antibacterial ointment. Back at camp, I change into my end-of-day clothes—a soft cotton T-shirt, clean leggings, light flip-flops—and properly dress my wounds with sterile bandages. The table, I realize, is a godsend. It lets me elevate my injured leg, gives me a flat surface to make dinner within reach, and supports my aching body as it keeps it clean, off the ground, and out of the dirt.

After dinner, I limp over to the dumpster and get rid of all the garbage I've been holding onto for days. Trash is weight, so the ability to lighten my load is yet another unexpected bonus of staying here. I take advantage of the vault toilet's convenience, too. Back at camp, I cautiously slide my bruised ass onto the bench of the picnic table.

"Some wild woman you turned out to be," I mutter, taking stock of my tame surroundings.

I spread both arms out wide across the picnic table, giving them a good stretch. Then I place a sunburned cheek on the table's cool surface and close my eyes. Tears slide down my sideways face, pooling in the hair at my temple. "I love you, picnic table," I whisper, giving it a pat with my hands. When I raise my head again, I see the campground with fresh eyes. "Thank you, campground," I say in a clear voice for anyone to hear.

I take a long time brushing my teeth to avoid going to bed. The inevitable pain of bending low to climb into my tent triggers the nausea I felt earlier. I spit into the bushes, take a deep breath to steel myself, and gingerly crawl into my tent. I am growing stiffer by the hour, and if it took this long to crawl into my tent, I wonder how long it will take to break camp in the morning. How long it will take me to hike a mile, let alone 400 more. *Will I be able to hike at all? Is my trip over, right now?*

To take my mind off that worry, I refocus on my bedtime routine. This is when I usually take care of my feet, but I'm so mad at them right now I want to skip their nightly massage. I look down at my innocent bare feet, completely unscathed from today's serious fall. They are in great shape—no blisters, no strains, no black toenails or broken bones. I have asked a lot of my feet on this journey. They have been so strong, and it's not fair to punish them for growing tired. For being imperfect.

I brush away a tear, grab the healing balm from my pack, and begin to rub my feet. The gentle touch, the extra pampering they deserve tonight, has been a long time coming.

When I was a little girl, my mom took me to an orthopedist who prescribed hard-soled corrective shoes with rigid insteps that dug into my tender arches. Square snapshots from the '70s capture me in blonde pigtails wearing tiny white leather boots that look like stiff ice skates without blades. The awkward high-tops hurt my feet, but they didn't stop me from running wild on our farm in central Iowa.

After I outgrew the high-tops, I was laced into a pair of corrective saddle shoes that I wore to kick rotten apples down the driveway, flip dead animals over with a curious toe, and unsuccessfully jump across the ditch of dark liquid runoff from the hog lot.

"You look like a street urchin," Mom had declared as she marched me by the elbow to the front porch, leaving me alone on the cold concrete step with a rag and a bottle of Kiwi polish. Resigned, I pulled a saddle shoe off one foot, lifted the tongue, and shoved my small fist up its throat to hold it in place as I whitewashed the pig shit and scuff marks.

Once I grew out of the saddle shoes, my feet still turned in a bit, but not enough to warrant a third pair of expensive custom orthotics. I loved the freedom of running barefoot and wiggling my toes in the cool grass of our front yard. Even the hand-me-down canvas tennies I got to wear felt like heaven. But Mom was not content with my slightly imperfect feet, and without the rigid shoes to bind me, she assumed their unforgiving role in my life. Throughout my preteen years, Mom would walk behind me at the shopping mall or in the grocery store, scrutinizing my body's flaws, digging into tender places. "You're toeing in again, Becky. Straighten out that right foot," she'd say. "It's for your own good, you know. Don't you want to look pretty?"

What I desperately wanted, more than anything, was for her constant corrections to stop. So, I learned to walk straight like a good girl—craving her approval, and watching her pride in me grow, with each painfully molded step toward perfection. I learned to navigate the world through her eyes, by her training. I became good and fixed, pretty and pleasing. No longer able to run wild.

* * *

I COULD FEEL MOM'S eyes on me today, watching and correcting my stride, shaming my imperfect feet on the trail. My mom may have contributed to my body-image issues, but it's up to me to reject the notion that my flaws are sources of shame and need to be fixed.

"Thank you, feet," I say, giving each a squeeze before carefully tucking them into the toe of my down sleeping bag. "I'm not going to correct you anymore. You are amazing just the way you are."

I carefully slide the rest of my body into the bag, wincing as I pull the zipper. Outside, the campground is growing dark and quiet. There are no generators, no twinkle lights, no loud music, no bears rummaging through trash. In the quiet of my small tent, alone with my thoughts, I can feel every scrape and tender bruise. My pulse throbs at every point of impact.

I think about little Becky, who just wanted to explore her curiosity. Instead, she was taught that running wild was unattractive, that flaws needed to be corrected. Her feet were bound.

It's hard to get comfortable on my air mattress, so I wiggle my toes.

"I'm sorry," I whisper to my younger self, "for not standing up for you then, but I'm here now. I know it was you who brought me out here, back to explore the wild. Thank you."

An image of another kid, Sunglasses, floats into my head. He's probably not much older than my sons back home. I doubt my own boys would know what to do, or how to respond, if a strange woman fell down and snarled at them. I feel really bad about what I said to Sunglasses.

It hurts to shift positions in my sleeping bag, but I have to.

"I'm sorry, Sunglasses," I say, making amends to the east side of my tent, in the direction of the railroad exhibit. "It's not your job to rescue me because you're a guy, or to soothe my wounded pride. I can see now that you tried to reach out to me, but I was too insecure to hear you. I see myself in you, Sunglasses, when you fixed your hair in the car window and hid behind your dark lenses. It's hard to admit we care what people think of us, but we do."

I continue to toss and turn, uncomfortable in my injured body. Restless about what the new day will bring and if I'll be up to the challenge. I have another pass to climb tomorrow, and many more to climb after that. I am feeling crushed. Not just by the thought of having to go home early. I'm more troubled by my behavior during my potential last day on the trail. I don't want to go out this way. I don't want the trail to remember me like this. I don't want to be a badass if it's just an image and a list of adventures I post to Instagram. That's not being a badass, that's just me being an ass. I roll over with a groan, and try to sleep.

The early morning is calm and cool as soft light and birdsong filter into my tent. Despite a terrible night's sleep, I'm ready to climb out of my sleeping bag and start the day. One twinge from my hip, and the details of yesterday's fall come flooding back; I freeze, anticipating spikes of pain. But they never come. I'm pleasantly surprised by how good I feel, considering. Cautiously, I test my left arm, then a leg. They are stiff, true, but a lot better than I thought. I think I'm okay.

I unzip my sleeping bag and get dressed for the day. When I put on my socks, I can't help but smile. "Good morning, beautiful feet."

As I wiggle all ten toes on my perfectly imperfect feet, something dawns on me. I have been trying to do this hike to perfection. From how I look on the trail, to the way I walk down the trail. All the nasty inner bullying, making self-corrections at every step, is actually sabotaging my trip and ruining my life. It's not just the need to be perfect; the need to be *seen* as perfect is all-consuming.

When you have an addiction, the first step is to admit you have a problem.

"My name is Becky, and I'm a perfectionist," I say to the birds as I pack up my tent. I try to do a slightly sloppy job, but it's hard. One step at a time.

Picking yourself up after you fall is an important trail lesson, because it happens to everybody. It's only natural to stumble sometimes. Perfectionism is exhausting. Carrying insecurity around is a heavy load. Like a pack weighed down with extra garbage, it can make the fall worse, make the injuries more painful. By the time I shoulder my backpack, the campground is beginning to stir.

I am tired and bruised, but all the more reason for me to get moving. I can do this.

As I leave Kenosha Pass, a breeze whispers through the aspens, brushing heart-shaped leaves against one another, hearts against hearts, in the most delicate wind chime. The trees' classic white trunks reveal black browsing scars made by hungry elk, proving that old wounds can heal. It's these random scars that make each tree different, that make aspens so iconic and beautiful. The beauty is in the natural imperfections.

Don't you want to look pretty.

In my experience, prescribed beauty is pretty painful. Imperfection is our natural state, and to be in our natural state is to be wild and beautiful. It's letting go of the social conditioning that teaches us to be perfectionists and pleasers. Perfectionism is our cage. Our hobbling. It's busywork that distracts us from being truly engaged in life. If wild means natural, authentic, just being who we are, then my way of being wild is to stumble a bit through life. And that's okay.

I want to be a badass only if it means I'm living wild on my terms, free of all the self-condemnation that dogs each and every step a woman takes. I look down and accept my feet as I understand them— imperfect and strong. If any feet can take me to the end of this long trail, I trust these two to do it. Their flaws keep me humble. Stumbling keeps me on my toes.

The journey of a 500-mile trail begins with one awkwardly wild and pigeon-toed step. "Let's go, feet!" I say to the beaten-up trail runners below me, always at the ready. "There's another pass to kick our ass today. Time to make tracks."

Hooves at the Precipice

Jacqueline Sheehan

WHEN YOU ARE ON A WRITING RETREAT WHERE YOUR BED IS IN A TREE HOUSE, in a lantern-lit encampment hemmed in by jungle and ocean, and the village is accessible by boat or a rocky coastal path that only horses or burros can maneuver, it seems like anything is possible. At least that's what I was hoping. In one month, my oldest sister had died suddenly, my divorce was final, my daughter left for college, and I found a lump in my right breast. The lump turned out to be gristle, but there was no changing the rest of it.

I had been on other writing retreats around the world, but this one was by far the most remote. We arrived by boat, unburdened by life jackets, and leapt into the surf to find our way to the shore. We slept in platforms in large trees and had been sternly warned about scorpions. Donkeys bellowed from sunset until three in the morning, at which time the parrots rose from the jungle canopies with a shattering series of screams until sunrise. At dawn, the village dogs woke up and barked. All of them. I came here to write and relax. I had not slept in four days.

I was in Yelapa, Mexico, fifteen miles southwest of Puerto Vallarta. Everything about this village on the Bay of Banderas murmured a steady promise of change, prodded me with the opportunity to be the person I wanted to be, if I could only figure out who that was. Every morning when I woke up, I felt further from who I believed myself to be. A psychologist. A writer with a first book dangling by a lifeline. Was there a sign that I had missed along the way? Would I ever feel the surge of desire again?

We were here for one week to write, but the afternoons offered our intrepid group the chance to explore. Yelapa was the very place that Bob Dylan and Dennis Hopper came for inspiration, and in my state of fever dream weirdness, I hunted for any remnants of their leftover muses. In fact, I would have grabbed at anything that left me feeling less mealy.

When I heard that three writers had scheduled a trail ride into the jungle with a waterfall destination, I took it as a sign. I was a terrible horseback rider; the large animals frightened me. What better way to wake up from the internment camp of death and divorce than to challenge a primal fear? I wanted the trail ride to the waterfall. Jared, an ex-pat with a golden mare, was our trail guide.

Ramon brought the horses from his stable in the village and he quickly summed me up. He handed me the reins to a small horse that looked beaten down from hauling everything from firewood to butane tanks. In Yelapa there were no cars because there were no roads, and horses were truly beasts of burden.

"This horse is muy tranquilo," he said in the mix of English and Spanish that moved commerce along.

I wondered if he meant exhausted. But tranquility was an ancient cornerstone of this village. Even Cortes, when he came ashore in 1524, was so taken aback by the tranquility and peacefulness of the indigenous people that he spared them the fate of enslavement. To this day, the original residents still reside on, own, and control their own land.

But tranquil or not, my horse was a worker, un campesino. Ramon gallantly gave me a nudge to help me up on the horse. The stirrups on my dark horse, whom I quickly named Tranquilo, did not match; one was metal, the other was wood. It's not like there was a tack store for equestrian supplies in the village. And the stirrups could not be adjusted. My feet didn't exactly dangle, but I was sure that more than just my toes were meant to settle in the stirrups.

The other three riders had either lived in Wyoming or were sent to dude ranches as teenagers. They swung their legs over the horses like pros.

I'd ridden horses before and I never advanced beyond terrified. I took lessons briefly in our sixth-grade Girl Scout troop, long enough to earn one horsey badge. On a trail ride in Kauai, I was assigned a horse with a menacing stare, who tried hard to scrape me off his back in trees and along fences. There was never a moment when I wasn't clenching my stomach, my hands sweating.

In general I was sure that horses didn't truly want humans astride their backs. I seriously doubted that they wanted a metal bit in their mouth. Who would? At any moment they could stage a horse revolt. I would, if I were a horse. All of which was in conflict with my desire to ride into the wind, gallop along the crest of a hill.

Who hadn't heard about horses' power of sensing a person's emotions, with fear being at the top of the list? I knew my horse would be better at reading me than I would be at reading him. Or at least I hoped that this was the gist of our wordless conversation as our group saddled up at the retreat center.

Even the first steps out of the primitive retreat center looked treacherous. Going down a hill looked far worse than going up a hill. And we had to go down to get to the main trail. My body arced in fear as we descended the rock and tree-rooted trail leading out of the village.

I made a choice. Tranquilo and I needed to open up a line of communication. If you're a writer and live in a land of magical realism, communicating psychically with an old horse is not that hard.

Tranquilo said, "I have gone this way one thousand times. See this boulder? This one's name is Juanita; she kisses my hooves each time I touch her. Watch me, and feel me carry you."

I chanced to tilt my pelvis to see if there was room to move without falling off. A less gracious horse would have rolled his eyes at my hesitancy. Tranquilo responded by giving me more space. My sit bones squawked. He said, "Oh, me too. Here, let's tilt together. There that's better." Fortunately our psychic language was in English.

And so we started, down the trail, following close to the others, past the village palapas made of banana leaf and palm, past the open fires in front of each family, water boiling in pots, past the women washing clothes in the wide shallow river, and the skinny short-haired dogs bristling at attention as we went by. The air smelled of wood smoke, dung, and the rich scent that came directly from Tranquilo.

I should say that he was not the most handsome of horses. He was filled with flaws of a lifetime, nicks and scars. I feared that if I put my glasses on and looked at his skin, I would see worse than that. I decided not to examine closely, not that he would have minded. He was beyond such embarrassment, but I chose to offer him the illusion of sleekness, of rippling flank muscles and a shining coat. I picked a burr out of his mane.

We left the palapas and went suddenly and alarmingly up a steep incline. The narrow trail hugged a hill on the right and on the left was oblivion, a deep canyon dotted with boulders. When I looked over the edge, I was so shocked that all my ligaments spontaneously weakened and my stomach turned upside down. I pictured my crumpled body at the bottom of the canyon. But Tranquilo pulled us up with surprising strength. I flattened my torso over his neck and prayed. This location lodged in my brain as the place of terror that must be revisited if we were to ever return from our journey. It etched on my skin in deep blue and red tattoos and stayed with me all day. All my fear focused on the dread of going down the sharp, steep corner, the unimaginably bouldered trail. It was also where I was going to dismount and crawl on all fours rather than ride downhill.

We continued to go up and up, along rivers, sometimes down, but mostly up. I spoke to him in bits of Spanish every time he pulled us up through a difficult passage. "Muy bueno," I murmured and I stroked his neck. I experimented with micro-movements left and right, forward and backward, leaning back when Tranquilo pitched downward, forward when he pulled into a climb. I felt the steadiness of his pace, Tranquilo's personal rhythm.

He knew everything about the trail, everything. When one of the horses took off into the trees, Jared, our trail guide, told us, "*You have to be the one in control; the horse must know that you are the one in charge.*"

I was not in control of my life and not the least bit in control of this horse. That was just not so with Tranquilo and me. I didn't even know the right questions to ask. This was his world, not mine. I let him drive.

We arrived at the waterfall, and I would like to say it was worth the dusty, arduous ride. But even the refreshing pool of water seemed irrelevant. Something else was scratching at my brain as we swam, ate, and scribbled away in our notebooks.

The thought of the return trip stripped all the glisten from the waterfall. We saddled up again. The majority of the return journey was going back down.

After an hour, Tranquilo descended a steep and purely boulder-covered passage that looked impossible. I panicked when he was busy picking his way, and I did something, I don't know what, clenched, leaned forward, but I nearly caused us to stumble. At the bottom, he sighed, heavy breath flapping his soft lips. This was his ultimate show of displeasure.

"I'm sorry," I said in our psychic lingo. "I wasn't ready."

Then he did this amazing thing. Right before the next steep decline that looked even more improbable than the last one, he stopped and gave me what I needed, a space to get ready. He felt me adjust, sit back, and then, and only then, did he go on. He understood the exact places where I needed more time. Call me delusional, but he offered me a kind of acceptance that I hadn't felt in years.

As we approached the place of terror, I tried everything. Relaxation, imagery, I dragged out level-two Reiki, summoned the Reiki masters.

Tranquilo said, "It is possible that you don't need so much extra baggage with us."

But I was losing faith. I pictured the dreaded place and

wondered how it would feel when Tranquilo and I spiraled off the cliff. It will take hours for help to be summoned, for a boat to arrive.

As we passed through a deceptively flat stretch of trail, I heard the rapids ahead. I could already feel the earth falling away. The corner, the precipice was up ahead, the one etched with landmarks in my still intact skull. The moment that Tranquilo and I turned the corner, there would be nothing below me, only open space, unattached. This is how I would die. Tranquilo maintained his pace as if there was no disaster ahead. Had he forgotten? In the last second, I gave him every bit of my faith and I stayed with him.

But what was this? This was not the vast cliff, the spot of death-defying danger. Tranquilo and I had already stepped over a hundred places much worse than this. Had there been a warp of time and space? This spot was nothing.

"Yes," said Tranquilo. "I could have told you but it would not have been the same."

I could not have imagined that I would have loved him this much, this worker horse. At trail's end, I slid off him with reluctance and gratitude. I fished around in my pack for anything that I had to give him and found an apple core. With all the sweet grace that was his nature, he accepted it.

I will never ride a galloping stallion over the crest of a hill with the wind in my hair. I'm a terrible horseback rider. But for one day through the jungle, Tranquilo was my gleaming stallion.

That evening when my lantern was turned down, I slept to the pure melody of burros, their nocturnal arias bouncing off the mountain wall, cloaking me with warm notes. The green parrots took over and entered my dreams at the appointed time, soothing me with tales of hope and faith. Howling dogs brought in the sweet dawn. I felt a warm ember of hope tucked under my ribs, and felt the steady clomp of Tranquilo's hooves matching my heartbeat. Somewhere out there, Tranquilo was waking up. And so was I.

On the Outside, Moving On

Nora Bonner

THE MORNING AFTER I GOT OUT OF PRISON, THE FIRST THING I DID WAS WALK through an intersection while the light was red. The cars were stopped but I was moving, even though every magnetic pull in my body tried to halt my legs and feet. The night before I'd stayed at a shelter in a room for women but it was so strange, knowing that men were on the other side of the building. I hauled a garbage bag full of notebooks I'd filled during my ten years inside, dreaming of who would eventually read what I'd jotted down, not knowing that I had no idea where to get started. Not just with finding readers for my notes from prison. Get started with anything.

So many American dream stories start with, "I arrived with twenty dollars in my pocket." The state of Georgia gave me sixty. I had no idea what to do with it. Get myself to a library so I could apply for a job? Get myself to a thrift store to find another outfit?

I had no family still talking to me to pick me up, so I relied on a GED teacher's kindness to get me back to the city. She agreed to drop me off at the Salvation Army where I didn't sleep because I've never been so afraid in my entire life. I had no one to return home to. All I had when I went in was a mother and a half-brother, but neither lived in Georgia, where I was sentenced to serve parole. My mother still lived in Virginia. My half-brother lived in Saginaw, Michigan. I didn't know how to contact either of them, and if I had, I don't know if I could have put them through the decision of whether they should reconfigure their lives, abandon what they're doing, move back south and start over just for me. It's hard enough for just one person to start over.

I walked through that intersection at the end of the block away from the shelter, and as I stepped between the rows of daffodils dividing the eastbound lanes from the west, a car honked. It took me a moment to realize that the honking was at me, but when I did realize it, I panicked. It was like someone doused me in a bucket of sound and I was so wet and cold I couldn't move. All bad things in my life start with a car honking at me. Start with a man honking at me in his car. You look like you could use a ride. [Ignore.] Where're you headed?

[Keep your head down. Move along now. Move it, move. Move-move-move.]

But I couldn't keep my head down and I couldn't move. I gazed right at the guy sticking his head out the window.

Hey, you all right? You need a ride? He wore sunglasses and a Falcons cap. You got a name?

The light turned green and he sped away. I could move again, but I couldn't because now the traffic kept me there. I couldn't move because twelve years ago I got into a guy's car and lost my life. I was sixteen, running back to the home I'd snuck out of so I could attend a party. Running away from that party because Harper Kennedy had spread a rumor that I was a lesbian. Funny now, because I've kicked it while locked up with five or six girls and honestly, it was no big deal. But it was a big deal to me that night when I was sixteen and I hadn't even had my first kiss.

It was about eleven at night when I'd gotten into that guy's car and went home with him. His name was Greg and he was seventeen and a dropout. He took me down to Atlanta, where the two of us fucked on narcotics. I aborted his baby. Five months later, I found myself charged as an accessory to a crime I'd actually slept through. A year later I pled guilty to reduce the charges to ten years instead of the rest of my life. Ten years later I'm out with a felony label and stopped at an intersection because I can't move.

Nobody tells you this stuff. When you're inside, I mean. When you're sleeping on a mattress, fingernail thin, with your shoes on because one of the girls in your dorm is mad at you and likes to steal people's shoes for revenge, only to return them full of spit or chewed up bread or excrement or something else to ruin them. When you're sleeping with your shoes on to protect your shoes, it doesn't matter if someone tells you how hard it will be out there on your brain because your body craves anything but that place. But still, they don't tell you. But still, there is no way to prepare, even if they gave you an entire encyclopedia set of information about what it's gonna be like out here.

The lights turned red again and the walking figure glowed. I pictured a face on him. I pictured lips saying, Move along now. Move move move.

I moved along because I had to. It's amazing what you can do because you have to.

I WALKED MORE MILES that day than my feet could count before spending a month in the back of a church in the heart of the city's expensive neighborhood. I found it while wandering around. Their playground was open, and for a little while, I slept in the yellow plastic slide connected to a blue and pink plastic playscape. This was fine during the summer months, when the plastic didn't turn cold. It heated up, though, because the slide was right in the sun, and I couldn't sleep in too long. This, too, was for my benefit.

I am not a person of the kind of faith that church practiced, nor am I a person with the kind of income the average attendee tithed for that church. I don't know how a person gets faith or money. I never had any, even before I was locked up.

Like I said, I slept in that slide for about a month before one of the janitors at the day school found me in there. She had to come in early one morning, to pick up after some kind of party or something they had in there for prospective students' parents. Her name was

Gloria, which made me smile because I, too, have a G name and I have always felt oddly connected to people whose names start with G.

The church was a white church in a white neighborhood, but Gloria was a Black woman with ten grandchildren split between four grown children. She told me all this the first time she brought me breakfast, which I ate on a bench on that playground. She reminded me of one of the chaplains at the prison. By that I mean, she had a kind of no-nonsense toughness to her that I'm pretty sure was a defense mechanism. She told me that I'm not the first person to ever make a home in that slide, but it was too dangerous to sleep there. Even a pretty girl like you, she said. Somebody might call the cops.

That's when I told her I'd been locked up.

She put me in touch with somebody who was in charge of the white church's ministry to help poor people. That person hooked me up with a job painting house interiors all over the city—one that specifically "second chance" hires folks with the felony label. The job gave me enough money to rent a place with one of the other painters, Gabby, another woman with a felony whose name starts with G. We don't mind painting. We don't mind living together, though we stay up all night learning how to read tarot cards, hoping that they will tell us if there is anything else for us out here besides painting. Something with better healthcare.

LAST WEEK, I WAS driving by that old neighborhood with the church and I parked the car and stepped on the playground. It was a Sunday, after the service, when most people had cleared the building. Still, the back door was open, so I went inside to see if I could find Gloria or someone who knows Gloria. I went upstairs feeling like a dirty intruder, but I didn't feel unsafe. It helps that I am a white girl and I know where to find new clothes at consignment stores that could fool anyone that I haven't spent a day in prison, or would have been able to if there was no such thing as a search engine.

At the top of the stairs, there was a conference room with the door open. I was about to turn around and head back to my car when somebody, a young guy, called to me: Hello?

I'm sorry, I called back. I was just looking for somebody.

Who are you looking for? he asked.

Gloria Jenkins, I said.

I don't know a Gloria, he said.

She's talking about a janitor at the day school, somebody else said: a lady with salt and pepper hair tied up in a yellow scrunchie. She stood up and spoke to me from the landing. I'm sorry, she said, but Gloria's moved on.

I wasn't sure if that meant that Gloria had died or had found another job, and I was afraid to ask. I wasn't in the mood to be devastated. I never am. I've had enough devastation to last me a lifetime.

Who are you? the scrunchie lady asked.

My name is Genna, I said. Five years ago Gloria helped me. Actually, your minister helped me, too. I forget his name. He found me a job.

The words came out in spurts of stuttering, which was weird, because I'm not the stuttering type.

I'm Linda, the lady said.

I told her it was nice to meet you but before I could get away, she asked if I'd ever attended a service. I tried to say no without showing I never planned to.

Sounds like God found you through this church, the lady said. Doesn't that make you wonder if you should attend a service?

I'm not that type of a person, I said. I just wanted to tell Gloria thank you because she changed my life.

I'm sorry you missed her, Linda said. But I believe we might still have her phone number on record.

I was so damned relieved, let me tell you.

Linda could see it on my face, I think, because she asked, Do you want me to leave a note for the secretary to pass yours on to Gloria?

I'd like that, I said, and gave her my cell.

A WEEK LATER, MY phone rang with a Virginia number and I thought it was my mother, but it was Gloria. She sounded exactly the same as I remembered her: soft and tough. I asked her what she was doing now and she said she was on disability. Is that good? I asked. Then I apologized, because what a stupid fucking question. I mean, I said, are you okay?

It's neither here nor there, said Gloria.

Hey, I said. Did you call me on a Virginia number?

I did, she said. Why'd you ask?

I thought you were my mother, I said. Then I said, in some ways, I guess you have been.

What's that now?

My mom lives in Virginia, I said. Then I told her, You saved my life.

She laughed. You said what now?

But Gloria knew she saved my life. I didn't need to tell her that, which was why she didn't need to acknowledge it to me. But I needed to acknowledge to her that I knew it.

Remind me which one you are again? she said. I recognize your name, but I can't put a face to it.

Genna, I told her. I'm the one who lived in the slide on the playground of that church in Piedmont.

There was a few of you, she said.

I'm the one who'd just gotten out of prison, I said, though it had been ages since I told anyone that about myself. I was almost mad that I did, because I was so close to forgetting it. I mean, I'll never forget it, but saying that again brought the experience closer to me than it had been.

Oh yeah, Gloria said, but I could tell she was just pretending to remember me.

She never asked me what my crime was, so I didn't ask her about her disability, though I was burning to know. I just wanted to tell you thank you, I said.

And plainly, she responded: You're welcome. And then we hung up. Sitting in my car in that white church parking lot, I felt the heaviness of someone who has been looked over for something they desperately hoped to receive.

I DROVE BACK TO the apartment, but Gabby was out. I sat at the table and drew a single card, a three of cups, from my tarot deck. It's the card for abundance. It's the card that means, "my cup runneth over." But it might as well have been the death card, because that's how I felt: like a skeleton who'd had her skin peeled off.

Right after that, Gabby came in from the corner store with a bottle of wine, but I'd quit drinking. Something she was well aware of. What are you doing with that, I asked her. Mocking me?

You said you'd drink again if you had something to celebrate, she said.

Oh yeah? Well I don't. I pushed the empty glass across the turquoise cloth over our two-person table.

Yes, you do, she said. We're having a baby.

By that she meant she was having a baby and she expected me to help. Doesn't look like you should be drinking either, I said.

I'm just having a couple of sips, she said. The rest is for you.

I never did have much self-control, so I let her pour me a glass. First glass I'd had since December. Now it was April and we had peach blossoms smashed against the window behind our sink. The sun pinked them and oranged the rest of the pane. It felt like something to celebrate so I sipped and imagined what our kitchen would be like with a toddler tearing through it. I pictured the two of us laughing at a little girl sitting in a high chair with purple icing from her first birthday cake spread across her cheeks. That image felt like something to celebrate.

Who the fuck is the father? I asked as I finished my glass.

Who the fuck cares? said Gabby. We laughed and laughed, and when she pulled the death card out of the tarot deck, we laughed even harder. I think you got my card and I got yours, I said.

No way, she said as she poured me another glass. I love this card. This card is like the restart button on the original Nintendo, she said and again, we laughed.

Her presence across the table felt warm, the table felt warm, and the warm light all made me feel like a skeleton staring at its next set of skin. That, too, felt like something to celebrate, which we did, even if we would never feel we'd be able to afford any of it.

That thought reminded me to ask, Did you play the lotto today?

Gabby widened her eyes with remembrance and pulled a scratch card from the back pocket of her jeans. I handed her a dime from the back pocket of mine, but she shoved the card in my hand and said, No, you. You're the one who drew the three of cups.

She stood over my shoulder, leaning on the kitchen counter as I scratched away. We never win anything, but that evening, Gabby had bought a card that won her two thousand dollars toward the abundance we'd spend on her baby. It wasn't a lot, but it felt like a fortune. Something to celebrate.

Inviting Her In

Peter Young

YOU THINK YOU'RE SO BOLD.

You should keep your ugly mouth shut.

Janet lies on her back in bed, her eyes closed, trying not to listen. She focuses on her breath, imagining it going all the way down to her toes.

Julian's going to leave.

The last thought smarts. Janet sits up and checks the time on her phone. It's an hour and ten minutes before her friend Anna arrives. She yells for Maslow, their wirehaired terrier mix, even though she knows he went with her husband. For a second she fills with joy thinking about his black eyes and scrubby off-white fur. She giggles at how her husband calls him Tater because of his tater-tot-shaped body and stubby legs.

Sensing a cruel thought about to pounce, she declares, "I can do this," and jumps out of bed, adopting a new strategy: stay busy and run out the clock.

Janet showers and while drying off squeezes the skin on her hip bone. It feels like a lot. She wipes steam off a full-length mirror and turns to the side to see some puckering of skin on her backside. Cellulite. She rotates her body seeking out more. Realizing what she's doing, she marches out to get dressed.

In the kitchen, she makes coffee and while sipping it prepares a vegetable and cheese frittata. She tells herself she won't have any. After putting it in the oven, she cuts up fruit. This she can have.

In the dining room, she clears the table of three days of mail and dirty plates. There's a mirror on the backside of the hutch cabinets. She opens it and pulls down two wine glasses to get a glimpse of her face and neck. She's relieved they look thin.

She walks through the house opening curtains. In the living room, she stands in front of the big window and looks out hoping to see her friend. It's an overcast March day, but along the block, all the trees explode in vibrant green. Across the street, a child in dingy, gray clothes and long, dark hair stares in Janet's direction. Janet leans forward, adjusting her glasses, and squints to bring the figure into better focus. She gasps when she sees the gaping hole in its face.

"No!" she hisses and yanks the curtains closed.

She checks the time on her phone. "I can make it," she tells herself. "I can make it." She marches to the kitchen and gathers plates and silverware. While setting them out on the table, she hears a knock. Tiptoeing up to the front door, she looks through the peephole. To her relief, it's her friend. She opens the door and shouts, "Yay! It's you."

Anna cries, "Yay. It's you too," and throws up her arms. A short, muscular woman, tattooed purple and brown swallows swoop up one arm and down the other. Anna, like Janet, is in her late thirties and has a few strands of silver in her wavy dark hair.

They hug, and Janet pulls her friend inside, scared about what might appear in the street. After closing the door, she draws her eyes down to Anna's belly, claps, and places both hands on her stomach. "Any kicking?"

"Oh, stop," Anna playfully slaps Janet's hands away. "I'm just six weeks."

"But I'm sooo excited!" Janet grabs her friend's hands and swings them side to side. "Wait. Where's Harris?"

"Since Jules is out of town, I said I wanted you all to myself."

"Bonus," Janet belts.

They walk into the dining room and sit down at the table. For several minutes, they share stories about their lives; Janet, a high school counselor, has a kid from an apostolic family who just came out to her. Anna says she's going to keep doing massages up until the last minute. Janet shares she just spread compost on the garden. Anna says she's inheriting a bassinet and a ton of reusable diapers.

When the timer dings on the oven, not wanting to lose a second with her friend, Janet races into the kitchen. She pulls the frittata out, steam fogging up her glasses, and drops it on the stove top.

After sitting back down, Janet pulls her feet up under her thighs and leans in close. "Are you scared at all?"

Anna opens her eyes wide. "Oh, let me tell ya . . ."

Janet wiggles in her seat, anticipating something good, her haunting thoughts forgotten.

"A question has plagued me the last few days: How in God's name am I going to push something the size of a cantaloupe out from between my legs?" She holds her hands six inches apart on her lap and asks, her voice rising to a cry, "Tell me how?"

Janet shrieks, "I don't know!" and laughs until tears form in her eyes. After a gulp of water and a couple deep breaths, she asks her friend if she's had any morning sickness.

"One morning I was nauseous. Oh, but Harris opened some kimchi yesterday and I puked a little in my mouth."

Janet wrinkles her nose. "That rat bastard."

"That brings me to my new superpower," Anna crows, and describes her new sense of smell at length. "If there's one smelly sock in the whole house, swear to god I can find it blindfolded."

Janet taps her friend's wrist. "Is there anything stinky in my house?"

Anna purses her lips.

Janet sees the hesitation. "Wait. There's something? You can tell me."

"Well, it's not in the house but something smells super funky on the porch. I mean really bad."

Janet's stomach lurches. "Maybe there's a dead raccoon under the porch." Wanting to change the subject, she says, "Let's eat."

While bringing in the frittata she decides she's going to have some cheesy deliciousness. About to serve it up, she hears a knock at the door and freezes.

No. She wouldn't.

Another knock on the door. Janet cringes. Sensing Anna must be wondering who's there, she mumbles, "Must be a delivery," and goes into the hallway. At the door, she musters her courage and looks through the peephole. Just as she feared, her demon stands waiting on the porch. Tangled, greasy, dark hair obscures most of her ashen face save for the gaping hole where her nose and mouth should be. She looks up and sorrowful red eyes meet Janet's.

Janet shudders in dread and backs away.

The demon screeches.

"Is something going on?" Anna asks.

Janet stumbles into the dining room, trembling.

Anna leans forward in her chair. "Sweetie, what's the matter?"

"Nothing," Janet says, avoiding her friend's gaze.

The demon screeches again.

"Low blood sugar," Janet blurts, attempting to block out the noise from the porch. "I've only had coffee this morning." She sits down and serves breakfast, trying to keep her hands from shaking. In her periphery, a flash of black passes by the window.

Did she unlock the back door this morning? She's relieved Maslow's gone; he always freaks out.

"You're shaking," Anna says.

"I really need to eat." Wanting to take the focus off herself, Janet takes a bite of food. Distressed, she tastes nothing. Fortunately, Anna starts to eat, so the redirection worked.

The handle on the back door rattles. Janet chokes on her food. Coughing, she leans back to see if the back door's being opened. It isn't. It must be locked.

"Sweetie," Anna pleads, putting her fork down. "You've turned white."

Janet clears her throat. "I'm fine." A tapping on the window of the door starts up. "I'm fine," she cries to drown out the noise.

Anna grabs her wrist. "I'm about to call an ambulance. Talk to me."

Janet sits back in her chair and sweeps hair out of her face. "I just need a second."

The demon screeches. Janet jumps in her seat.

Anna points toward the kitchen. "What was that?"

Janet sighs and looks out the window. A thick, gray cloud cover hangs above the trees. "It's my demon." She rolls her head back to face her friend. "She wants in."

"Ahhh." Anna's mouth remains open as she gives one slow nod.

Janet heaves herself up and goes to the back door. On the other side of the window her demon, a lone yellowish fingernail touching the glass, stares up at her. Janet had forgotten how small she is. She's barely taller than the door knob.

Anna slips into the room and stands in the back.

Janet opens the door. "Come on in." She swings her hand wide behind her.

The creature sweeps in, long tangled hair covering her eyes and framing the gaping hole in her face. A putrid smell of something rotting trails behind. Janet gestures for the demon to follow her. She walks back to the table and pulls out a chair. Her demon sits down. Janet, nauseous from the smell, opens the window.

"I'll get you some toast," she tells her new guest and goes back in the kitchen. Anna, holding her nose, greets her just inside the doorway with a sympathetic look.

"I'm so sorry about the timing. As soon as she eats, she'll go away."

"It's okay, sweetie. Do what you have to do."

Janet opens a loaf of Julian's bread—she doesn't allow herself the simple carbs—and puts two pieces in the toaster. "You two have met, right?" she asks, opening a cupboard. She pulls down a bag of sugar and a jar of cinnamon.

"Never this close." Anna, still standing near the door, studies the demon. "But I have to say, mine seems scarier."

"Ha. Everyone thinks that."

"Her smell is so intense."

"Yeah." Janet makes a sad face.

"It must make her feel safe," Anna suggests. "It keeps people at a distance."

"Sounds about right."

"What did it take for you to start inviting her in?"

"Oh, god." Janet tilts her head back and looks up at the ceiling. "Let's see . . . as you know, two super-unwell parents, an ongoing eating disorder, a terrifically failed first marriage, and six years of counseling. But even now, as you just saw, my default is to ignore her."

Anna chuckles. "I know how that goes."

When the toast pops, Janet smothers butter on the pieces and sprinkles sugar and cinnamon over them. She cuts them in half and puts them on a plate. "Showtime," she says and walks back into the dining room and places the toast down in front of her demon.

Chortling, she picks up a piece with small opaque hands and pushes a corner into her gaping hole.

Janet sits down in her seat at the head of the table. She waves for Anna to join her. "It's going to be a few minutes. She takes her time."

Anna sits, waves the air in front of her, and leans in close to Janet, whispering, "Why is she here?"

"You don't need to whisper. She hears everything I do."

Anna rolls her eyes. "Duh."

"Well, thanks to me, we no longer have a place to live."

"What?" Anna cries.

Janet nods and takes a deep breath. "Thursday I got a letter from my landlord. Guess what? He raised our rent nine hundred dollars."

"Are you fucking serious?"

Janet, sucking in her lips, nods.

"Fuck that shit."

"I know, I know, but I thought, 'Oh, it's gotta be a typo.' So, I call him up and ask about it. He says, 'Oh, no. It's correct.'"

"Oh, no, it's correct," Anna mocks.

Janet raises a finger as well as her voice. "Apparently, he's not renting it at a 'fair market value.'"

Anna shakes her head. "The greed in this city is out of control."

"I reminded him we've been renting for three years and that a nine-hundred-dollar increase was, well, obscene."

"Oh, you go, girl."

"I mean, he can't need more money. He drives around in a new Audi for fuck sake."

"What did he say, what did he say?"

"He got real snide and said he's happy to rent to someone else."

Anna raises her middle finger and waves it around.

"So, I say, 'Fine, do that, cuz I'm not giving money to a parasite anymore.'"

"You did not!"

"I did," Janet squeals, clapping her hands. She abruptly stops and looks at her friend. "But now Jules is going to freak."

"You haven't told him?"

"I don't want to spoil his trip. He's so excited for this year's field study."

"Of course. That makes sense."

"But I'm terrified. He's not so good with his demons."

"Well, talk to him like you are now and have a few places lined up to look at."

"I've been looking!" Janet shrieks. She pauses to adjust her glasses. "Rent's out of control."

"It's like some people are possessed. They just can't get enough."

"And now I'm thinking, I shoulda kept my mouth shut. At least given Jules a say in the—" Janet is interrupted when her demon taps her empty plate with a fingernail. She continues tapping in slow, metered strokes. Janet locks eyes with her and memories sweep across her mind: her mother curled up on her bed having just said she ought to kill herself; her father passed out drunk, face down on the lawn, grass pushing into his mouth. And her, behind the barn, bent over and pushing two fingers down her throat. Beside her stand the horses Thunder and Abby with their ears forward, sensing her pain.

Janet, gripping the table, pushes herself up out of her chair. "She needs more."

She stumbles into the kitchen and drops bread into the toaster. She thinks about the horses being with her every time she made herself puke—never disgusted, never judgmental, always loving. She leans against the counter and presses a fist to her lips. Her eyes blur.

Anna comes into the kitchen and puts an arm around her. "Oh, Bunny."

"Whenever I feel super vulnerable, she always comes," Janet says, sniffling.

The tapping continues in the other room.

"It'll be okay." Anna rubs Janet's back. "We'll get through this."

A large tear slides down Janet's cheek.

Anna pulls her into a hug. Janet lets go and cries, the tears washing over her eyes like rain on a windshield. "Julian's going to leave me," she blubbers.

"No, he won't. He loves you," Anna says calmly, assuring her. "Besides, he knows I'll kick his ass."

Janet laughs and now her face is dripping with tears, snot, and saliva. She reaches behind her, yanks a dish towel off the stove, and wipes it off.

After dabbing her eyes, she sees a stain on Anna's shoulder and laughs. "Oh, honey, I soaked you." She finds a clean section of towel and presses it down on the wet fabric.

"Don't worry, it's practice. Better than milky spit-up."

Janet fills with joy at being reminded of Anna's expected baby.

"Oh, I wanna burp your liddle baby." Janet grabs her friend's arm and playfully tugs.

"Oh, you will . . . don't let the toast burn."

"Oh god, thanks." After preparing it, she takes it out to the dining room. The demon's no longer seated at the table. Janet walks into the living room. No one's there.

"She's gone?" Anna asks, having followed her.

"Yup." Janet goes out onto her porch and peers down both sides of the street. The demon is nowhere to be seen.

They return to the dining room table and sit down.

Seeing the frittata, Janet, now very hungry, picks up her fork and eats. Anna does the same. They eat for a while, an occasional scraping of a fork or slurp of the coffee interrupting the silence.

Janet pictures her demon and cringes at the gaping hole in her face. A moment later she softens realizing how utterly lonely the girl must be. She needs to be more kind to her.

Getting an idea, Janet turns to her friend, and excitedly taps the top of the table. "You know what?"

Anna, holding a cup of coffee, tilts her head, her eyes playful. "What?"

Janet pulls her feet up under her and claps. "Next time she comes I'm going to brush her hair."

"But she only comes when you're freaking out and then that freaks you out more."

"Oh, right, duh." Janet slaps her forehead and bows over laughing. After straightening up, she shoots a finger at her friend. "Okay, okay. I'm gonna *try* to brush her hair."

The Hunt

Anne Morales

WORKING QUICKLY BENEATH THE MOONLIGHT, SHE MOPPED THE SWEAT OFF her brow before picking up the old rusted shovel again. Silently, she pierced the thick clay soil and tossed it aside. Her shoulder ached, but she couldn't stop now. The leaves behind her rustled. She immediately threw herself to the ground and pressed herself into the earth, wishing herself invisible. After a few agonizing moments of nothingness, she forced herself to lift her head. An opossum, just a few feet from her, hissed before scurrying back into the woods. "Damn it," she cursed the creature as her heart still pounded in her chest. She stood up and began to dig again. Soon she found herself in a hole, now waist deep. "At least I have someplace to hide if they come," she bitterly smiled to herself.

Gnarled, barren trees lined the clearing she worked in, offering little to no protection if they came from above. The tall grass twisted toward her like fingers. Shivering, she kept digging. Deeper and deeper, one shovel at a time, she worked with machine-like precision. She paused a moment and stood in the eerie glow of the moon. In another time, this might have been almost beautiful, but now all she could feel was the fear pumping through her veins. She knew the consequences if she were caught, but she couldn't stay here anymore. It was too much to take.

In the moonlight, she saw the gravel start to shift, ever so slightly. Her eyes widened as the earth began to tremble and her blood ran cold. Right on cue, she heard the deep throaty growl of the engine firing up. As if forged from the bowels of hell, its roars reverberated for miles over the dark landscape. They were coming.

She fell to her knees and began clawing at the earth. She was so close to finding it! The roaring grew louder until it seemed to come from all sides. The ground shook so hard she thought the walls of the hole would collapse upon her, entombing her as a present for them. Tears streaked down her face as she felt the blood pounding in her head, but still she dug.

They were in the clearing now. The roar was deafening. Just as her ears felt about to burst, the engine cut off, leaving behind a sick silence in its absence that was so much worse. Sobbing, her hands flew as she threw the dirt behind her, now certain she was digging her own grave. She heard the boots pounding on ground getting closer by the second. She cried out in pain as her fingernail bent on something hard. It was the old metal trapdoor! She quickly brushed aside the rest of the dirt as a spotlight filled the hole, blinding her. Several shadowy sets of hands clawed at her as she ripped open the door and threw herself down a hatch.

She slammed the small door shut behind her and wove her arm into a ladder that descended down into something she would just have to deal with later. She fused her free hand to the rickety door handle as she felt them try to pry it open from above. She cried out as it opened a few inches, showing her the black of the boots and the cold steel of a rifle's barrel. She slammed it back down and turned the deadbolt lock so hard it sent shockwaves down her arm.

The spotlight from above oozed through the cracks in the trapdoor, violating the darkness accorded from below. She looked down for the first time, fully taking in the ladder's descent into the black abyss. Breathing hard, she shot one last glance up at the trapdoor. She heard the men's shouts and their fists beating on the door. They would not give up. "Whatever lies below must be better than what is above," she resigned as she began the descent into darkness.

A Distant Home

Nan Jackson

I remember how it beckoned—
The sheen of pre-dawn light
On the dark ocean.

I rushed headlong
Into deep water,
Swam far beyond
The moonscape slopes
Where sand dollars
Stood on edge,
Mossy and upright.
I dived down
Past familiar outcroppings of
　　coral,
Their surfaces rippling
Like dancers waving ribbons.
I passed the rocky crevice
Where I often saw
The ancient moray eel
Glimmering golden green.

All the way out
To where the continental shelf
Drops off
Where I once saw
Through the fog-like sameness
Outlines of hammerhead sharks.

I remember how I dived
So deep that nothing
Known to me
Remained.
Breaking all the rules—
No scuba buddy, no gauges,
No way to measure
Depth
Or time.

Serene and single-minded,
Weightless and wonderstruck,
I pushed myself
Farther than I'd ever been—
Becoming whole again.

Washed clean of past
And yet-to-come,
I looked up,
Like an astronaut
Seeing her distant home
For the first time.

I knew the risks
Of re-surfacing
And took the chance.

Untethered

Mary Kate Wilcox

"Turn here." The Big Dipper guides me tonight, and I guide him as
we roar over this land of seldom traversed memories. My fingers tap
against my thigh with restless impatience, giving in to the rhythm of
unbidden thoughts. How far till the water? It must only be a few miles
more, it has to be.

The dust flies up beneath the wheels, and occasional chips of
gravel knock hard against the windshield followed by his barely
audible curses. For a moment, he lifts his foot from the gas, allowing a
small spurt of deceleration. We float in limbo for those few slow
seconds, an odd place welling with the possibility of the pockmarked
road beneath us and weighed down by the stars.

Inevitably, we speed up again as we always do, hurtling on and
on to ease that nagging ache. My eyes wander through the dark
interior of the car to him, this boy sitting next to me. The sharp,
straight nose that overhangs the day-old stubble. His thin, delicate
hands clutching the wheel tightly as his red-rimmed eyes roam blankly
ahead. The emptiness startles me, though I wake up staring into those
eyes every morning and fall asleep haunted by the absent ghosts each
night. There is no recognition, no emotion at all. Just vacant orbs
reflecting the moon. I can almost see every bone poking out through
the thin coating of pale skin. Does he ache for anything? Does the
heartbeat in his chest register the infinite expansion of this moment
and the boundless pain when it deteriorates, crumbling into the past,

or does it simply thud on pumping static blood through his numb veins?

"You okay?" I ask quietly. The vertebrae bulge taught against the back of his neck as he nods. A skeleton coated in paper-mache. A piñata without a purpose hidden in the center. Just a mass of intricately constructed cardboard and plastered paper. The brown storms of dust vanish behind us, engulfing the eerily discerning eyeshine of startled deer. I imagine each particle of dust journeying back to the inky horizon. Swirling in invisible drafts and upwells of motion pulled onward by the intent of the sky. Maybe caught up in the miles of rusting barbed-wire fence and prickly sumac like the desiccated prey of a shrike, entangled not only in agony but in bitter irony, impaled by such an elegant, enchanting assailant. Or maybe escaping into the vast beyond, just out of reach.

Crimson and orange plumes of fire laugh as they race each other in uncontrolled lines across the prairie. The flames before me rise up in a deep, dark pink, shimmering in the night like salmon exploding up from the luminous depths of a far western river. The fire swims through the charred grass like a fish, gasping and shuddering, intricately and delicately tied to the matter it moves through.

The premature chuckling of a Carolina wren may fool me on brisk mornings when my breath just barely freezes in the dawn light, but the inferno crackling through the grass never will. Our Kansas volcanoes erupt and smolder only when spring flutters in on airy breaths. Perhaps she reads messages of longing in the sinewy tendrils of smoke? Or perhaps the crackling of the flame is an intoxicating love song summoning her back to us. The luminous fields of fire drown out even the stars tonight. Crackling gods of bright destruction and renewal delighting in a perfect incineration.

I have forgotten about the boy next to me till he shifts forward, spine bent in exasperation. His eyes squint with displeasure as I roll my window all the way down till I am drifting among the smoke that whirls through my lungs. Maybe he senses that just like Lady Spring, I too am hypnotized by the gentle summons of the flame and the smell of this smoke. The boy's love feels cold and icy after such flickering warmth.

A sandstorm of white dust swirls through the car as the gusty wind shakes the top layer of baking soda out of the Tupperware containers shoved haphazardly under the seat. I remember when he placed them there, so excited, so optimistic. "See, now no one can smell it, not even you."

How could I tell him that his clever idea was futile? That the rank smell of weed persisted on his clothes and his fingertips, not just in his car? That when he lays his damp head on my bare chest, the smell wafts through my nostrils, emanating even from his naked, freshly washed skin to sink into my pores, strangling me. How could I tell him that I woke up each morning choking and retching with his thin arms locked so tightly around me?

Brown coils of hair fly out into the darkness as I extend my head resolutely out the window. I can feel his hand inching toward the lever even if I cannot see it. Waves of annoyance pulse outward from him, manifested in the wafting clouds of white powder, as he yearns to close us off, to bar me from the haunting night sky. I gulp the scents of ash and flame and cattle into my nostrils with a rasping hunger, knowing I won't get such lung-filling, heart-stopping nourishment until next spring. A fish returned to the water just in the nick of time.

My hair whips my face with a million sharp lashes and my lips sting in the biting wind rushing past. The dry skin of my face burns, chapped by the fiery intensity of the air. My vision goes foggy as the soot fills my eyes but I resist the urge to scrub it away. The Flint Hills burn even brighter through the haze coating my sight. Indistinct mountains of flame rising up from the Earth and reaching toward the black sky. We cruise along in a strange, disturbed trance, composed of his irritation and my rapture. John Denver's voice lulls me into placidity. "Take me home, country roads." Yes, please take me home. "To the place I belong." Oh, John Denver, where the hell is that?

His hand jams the car abruptly into park, palm clenched tightly over the gear shift. The structure of his hand resembles the roots of a tree, long fingers snaking down to grasp the hard soil beneath, stationary, molded forever to the precious comfort below. We are here. The creek shines in the darkness. The Big Dipper gleams overhead, pointing me forward toward an indistinct dream.

My bare feet wobble precariously as I stumble down the slope of cracked and worn concrete. Pain shoots up into my heels but evaporates quickly in the thrill of the pulsating night. The headlights behind me blink and vanish, stranding us in darkness's arms. Night presses in with an exhilarating embrace and I limp on blindly, urgently, drawn to the water like the cattle that roam over the flickering hills looking for the ancient bison wallows flooded every spring, hoping to settle their weary limbs down in the ethereal pools.

The water laps at the rough, calloused edges of my toes, crisp as a glacial spring. Balance becomes an illusion, a fool's errand, on the submerged chunks of stone and partially dislodged cement below. The slope leading down to the water has disintegrated over time, depositing old cement among the river rock. Eventually, it will wear away into the perfectly formed stones below, but not yet.

Almost imperceptibly the road morphs into a smooth, low water crossing of limestone, so intricately placed eons ago. It has already lasted longer than the cement road on either side ever could. On warm summer evenings, old Chevy trucks and battered Fords will roar through the water, each trying to overpower the other's rumbling engine. Eventually, the drivers will stop, parked on the limestone top of the crossing, a new memory in this stone's unending consciousness. Their bulging bellies will exit the trucks first as they emerge, men formed by decades of Natty Light and unacknowledged discontent, to fish in the eddies below the waterfall, tumbling down just past the crossing.

The pebbles coating the crossing thrust into the soft, untested skin on the soles of my feet and I press my arches down onto the sharpness, waiting for a puncture. He calls for me back where he still stands next to the car, unending annoyance morphed into concern as he implores me to wait, begging caution, but I cannot. He yells from worlds away. The chilly water rushes over my toes as they glimmer bright and pale, some strange river creature straining against the current. The water transforms them into slender, graceful forms, like bluestem curved against the wind.

Finally, he meets me, where I wobble along the submerged crossing, savoring the momentary instances of stillness in my mind as my body rocks back and forth, servant to the uneasy balance of the pebbled layer below. I breathe easily because underneath those pebbles is a solid footing of limestone. If I fall, it will catch me. I will ache and bruise against its kind, unalienable certainty.

My body is hollow full of an echoing silence that vibrates through my ribcage. The river rushes forward in an animate dance. Water swirls like the smoke signals spiraling out over the burning hills. The messages drift upward to highlight the vague outlines of wispy clouds as they amble toward the moon. The thick brush rustles invisible on either bank and a great horned owl murmurs lazy remonstrances to the smoky sky.

His breath is drawn, ragged, and damp as he pauses beside me to look out at the "road" below our feet. I don't notice his closeness till he pants into my ear and the condensation gathers on my skin in moist droplets. He whispers, "We should go back now," and the lines of his palm intersect at sharp angles against mine as he grasps my hand, trying to pull me back the way we came. His skinny knuckles protrude out, gouging against my fingers. Does he not feel the stiffness of my hand against the wetness of his palm? His skin is heavy and overpowering and the water laps gently, softly, lovingly at my feet.

"Let's go." It is too dark to see his mouth form words but I can picture his disapproving face perfectly. He is anxious, prepared to humor me and sometimes indulge me but never to laugh with me. I can just barely see his eyes, worn and drained, lodged deeply in the sockets. The eyes of the summer fishermen, doggedly casting their lines out into the creek, waiting, just waiting for something to float along. Something that makes it all worth it. And then I remember their wives. The women aged beyond their years bobbing down the creek on gauzy plastic pool floats each summer. Parched mouths sucking on water-speckled cigarettes, the lit end illuminating the dark caverns of their gums at every draw. Their hard, accusatory eyes stare as their tattered children hurtle past, screaming obscenities at each other. The smell of cigarette smoke wafted through my airways that summer day as I treaded water in the creek, imparting the same feeling that curdles my insides each morning when I wake up, his dank arms bound taut around me.

With a deep sigh, I jerk my hand out of his, walking along till he is only a memory behind me. Barely submerged limestone becomes a deep, swift river with each step into the darkness. My heart beats in time with the coasting water's rush, clear and beautiful in the racing, shallow current but turbid and full of ominous potential as it descends further into the yawning depth of the night. These tendrils of air, water, and stone are guiding me far beyond him, into an ancient, elusive world. I breathe deeply, devouring the burning air with each inhale. The taste of ash flows from my nostrils to my tongue and I savor it as if the renewal of the springtime burns is lodged inside my body. Maybe, this spring shoots of rippling grass will burst from my innards in a spectacular emancipation. I can only hope. My eyes close as I step forward into the waterfall and off the crossing.

The waterfall is only half my height and when I stand, my head is still level with his feet above. The rocks below me glow in the darkness, slippery with the many universes of algae and moss wandering over their glossy surface. The certainty of the limestone crossing is gone. Now I stand among the unknown and the anxiety blooms inside my chest. It is an ugly feeling, crowding out the possibility of the dusky smoke, quashing the germination inside.

My feet scrape the sharp indentations and peaks of the boulders beneath me. I have no idea how big they are or how far into the Earth they extend. Is the riverbed miles below? Am I walking on the heads of slumbering, mineralized giants? What will happen when they wake and shake me off, throwing me into the unknown?

The boy stands above me on the crossing, worlds away, eons away, wary and unwilling to follow. A mutilated shadow unable to step out into the light. His outline blurs and shudders against my eyes. He remains rooted above me, an outline of a man etched by fear with red, dull eyes. He could be a ghost, except for the furious tension at his core, too solid to ever drift away into imaginings.

"C'mon, that's enough. Let's go back now." His voice is tired, edged with anger. At his words, the anxiety flares within me again. Soon it will overpower me, as it always does, and I will inevitably climb back up the waterfall and sit dripping water and sorrow onto the leather seats of his car. I will wake up trapped in his arms, roiling with nausea. The growth inside me snuffed out, tamed, no longer a wild prairie but a stagnant suburban lawn.

I push off from the boulder beneath me, flapping my arms in frantic strokes. "C'mon, that's not funny. C'mon, I want to go home." I can barely hear him shouting as I dunk my head into the invigorating water below. As I kick my feet, he shrinks behind me, the remnants of a bitter nostalgia no longer enough to moor me now.

I float untethered and alone, released. Branches rush by me or I rush past them, all of us unfettered, strange creatures. They loom alien in the night and resolve into dark shapes scurrying by. The branches could be joyous leaping fish or snakes writhing around my head. Their wake enfolds me, trapping me in the whorls and eddies of the current. I am farther downstream than I have ever traveled before and my insides expand blissfully against the water. My feet search and wriggle. I know that this will be the last mooring, the last spot I can touch in the darkness before the ground falls away. The rock is smooth. Maybe a weathered chunk of limestone or possibly the shell of a snapping turtle, I cannot tell which.

Back on the crossing, he flinches as my shirt splashes down

beside him. He stares with an unbelieving fury as the sopping T-shirt tangles on a jagged outcropping of cement. The boy is a vague outline but the tree roots of his hand clench and unclench as the folds of my T-shirt scrunch and compress, captive to an infinite pressure, bound to the cracked pavement by the continual movement of the water.

Leaves brush against my calves along with other unknown denizens of the liquid multitudes sprawling before and below me. I shiver, unable to stop my numb toes from clenching against the last comforting illusion of solid footing underneath.

I dunk my head into the water again, still frigid with echoes of winter. My lungs clench together as I open my mouth to engulf the gelid flow. Silt and silence swirl together against my teeth. Only the river can hear me now. I want to sink into the sublime murkiness running over my stomach, outlining the jagged stretch marks with a gentle hand. When I emerge, my hair streams out behind me, a creature longing to descend into that gaping maw of water beyond.

"Goddammit, this isn't funny. Let's go now. I said now!" His tirade is cut short as I fling my bra up in front of him, followed by my saturated jean shorts. He lunges for my bra but it floats merrily away from him, retreating into the untamed shadows only to be caught in the swirling tides near the muddy bank. My shorts lodge in a tangled mass of driftwood, evading the jagged edges of torn pavement and crushed rocks, fleeing the only tattered remains of normalcy left.

The water pushes against me, caressing my breasts in cold, gentle circles, embracing those parts of me I have always contained. The body that has never experienced the exhilaration of the night air, the smooth water, or the burning sun, that glorious world that my hands and face and feet take for granted. The fires on the horizon burn in thick lines over the Earth, a perpetual sacrifice, an eternal beginning. The thick band of scar tissue encasing my thighs tinges with heightened sensation at the cold flow of water passing over it. I am losing my footing on the unsteady mooring and I know that this is my last chance to swim back to him, that frothing phantom so far behind me.

The boy yells in shock as my underwear smacks him in the face and stumbles backwards to the edge of the crossing. Perhaps he could not see the dripping wad of fabric in the sojourn of night. The violent cursing and the harsh, meaningless bellowing grow faint as I extend my feet up toward the stars overhead, abandoning my perch below. My head lolls back into the current as I am sucked away. The water furls over the rolls of my body, excavating the world of curves and the blemishes, welcoming the scars and stretched skin as her own.

His form sinks from my view as I rise upon the river, simply another fragment in the infinite composition of this place, just like the moss lining the rocks or the disintegrating roots sagging against the bank. I drift away, my nakedness a sacrifice, the ultimate vulnerability in the sublime night. The wildness lines my body as it engulfs it. The immense mountains of fat, the deep valleys of muscle, and the hard outcroppings of bones are finally as reckless, unpredictable, and wild as the places I love.

The boy calls to me but his empty words vanish into the night. He belongs back there on the makeshift road that crumbles on either side of the low water crossing, so far away, and I belong to the water. To the pull of the stars and the wafting smoke above. To the lifeblood of the plains pulsing through the dark trees and the smoldering ash up on the hills. The Big Dipper guides me tonight as I ease into the flame rising over the prairie, into the multitudes around me. To the place I belong, an infinitesimal molecule drifting on an unending journey serenely out to sea.

Women Arise Now ~ Water to Fire

Genét Bosqué

Like Takanakapsaluk, we
have been sleeping
at the bottom of
the sea ~ our long hair streaming
in glacial drift.

We have believed
our position was
"under." We have been told
strength was meant
for men. We have thought
our beauty
was enough.

Now we arise!
And surfacing ~ we are
awake.

We are scrubbing
the old lies out
of our minds, scouring them
from our bodies ~ healing
in the radiance of

the sun. Now we arise
with our eyes opened
and clothe ourselves in
the light of our truth ~ strong and
wild, still beautiful, our
hearts aflame ~ love and valor blazing
from our faces.

Together we step onto
the road that leads
to self-discovery; *no one*
will avert us from our goal.

We arise from water with our
hair on fire ~ and we light
our own way
forward.

Bone Memory

Melissa Min

Middle age in me is taut and tamed,
The heart feels numb and the wild restrained.
Grief and shame keep desire at bay,
Resigned to stumble through most of my days.

But my Ancestors gather in the core of my heart,
Come, daughter, they whisper, *come back to the start.*
Restless and reckoning, in numbers they come,
All my old kin. And I am undone.

A woman sits and knits with ancient bones,
Hair of fly wire and eyes of stones.
A never ending blanket weaved from twine,
Emboldened with feathers and old teeth of mine.

Another smokes a pipe, with bells on her toes,
Lavender stems, silver ring in her nose.
White gossamer eyes, bones so fine,
Sorts diligently through old memories of mine.

A woman in lace with the voice of a crow,
Sits amongst everything I've ever disowned.
Lovers, lies, tangled knots of hair,
With quill and parchment, records them with care.

Old wise one with the mane of flame,
Self-appointed collector of all my shame.
Shows lost souls on dark corner streets,
Celebrates mistakes with all she meets.

My Mumma, false teeth and cigars in a tin,
Clutches faded photos with a loving grin.
My baby face in the image she holds,
Chews faithfully on secrets never retold.

Gran in pearls, white gloves and a purse,
Works hard to remove a family curse.
Her scent of bubbles and honeysuckle soap,
Oh my darling, she says, *don't you dare give up hope.*

They weep and sing and dream my song,
Barefoot at my side, they've been there all along.
A vigil they have kept from the very start,
Keening and crowing in the cave of my heart.

They speak in earnest of my sacred birthright,
To howl and dance by the full moonlight.
To commune with the *wild* that seeps from my bones,
To reclaim the self that I have long disowned.

I awake to the shimmer of a rising sun,
Everything in me is completely undone.
Clutching a simple, single white glove,
My heart filled with centuries of unfettered love.

Saint Iriana, the Cow-Herder

Red Hawk

In the village they called her simple,
by which they meant stupid, unfit
for any work but minding the Cows.

They laughed out loud at the way she
spoke to the Cows, as if they were
humans, royalty in fact. When they

were spooked by thunder or shadows
moving in the wind, with one arm
thrown across their wide shoulders

she talked them to the barn. Oh,
my dear Majesty, my kind Lord,
do not fear; I am here with you,

and to their amazement, the Cows obeyed.
At calving time, it was Iriana they called upon
to deliver. Only she could save the most difficult

of births. Oh Blessed among Females, you
are about to bring Our Lord to life, she murmured
to a Cow in difficulty, and she worked miracles.

But the villagers did not regard them as miracles,
could not bring themselves to believe that One
with dung-dried boots, who smelled like the barn and

talked to her Cows, that such a One as She
could have found, in their very fields,
a cud-munching, bellowing God.

A Married Woman Walks into a Bar

Lucy Jane Bledsoe

"DO YOU READ?" HERE SHE WENT AGAIN, TALKING TO STRANGERS, EXPRESSING every tiny insight as if it were a revelation.

The man blinked at Janis, his long blond lashes sweeping down and up, like a thought broom, one that said, *go away*.

Well, it was hardly a pickup line. He needn't get his hackles up.

"I'm here because of a short story I read in high school," she told him.

He nodded as if what she said made sense. It didn't. What *was* she doing here, in this seaside dive, belly up to the worn wooden bar, elbows planted like a regular, facing off with the head and neck of a giant twelve-point buck mounted on the wall above the bottles of spirits?

And yet Janis carried on. "A woman who's in this perfect marriage with money and four children can't bear her life and rents a motel room so she can sit by herself for a few hours every week. The thing is, she turns on the gas in the room and kills herself."

The man reached into his back pocket for his wallet to pay for his Coke.

"Doris Lessing. 'Room Nineteen.' My mother gave me the story when I was sixteen, and it was devastating. She told me it was exactly how she felt. It was like she'd punched me in the stomach."

Janis pressed her lips tightly to shut herself up. He didn't want to hear every twist and turn in her life story, for god's sake. Still, she wanted to tell him the next part, how, as the years went by, and she thought about her mom giving her that story, she got angry. Why didn't she go back to school? Get a job? Why the passivity? Janis vowed to never be that woman. The one in the story *or* her mother.

Janis sighed and heard herself start talking again. "What an arrogant twit, right? My mom shared the most private thought she'd ever shared with me, about wanting to kill herself, and my response was that I wanted distance. That I didn't want to be her."

The man shook back his blond, shaggy, adolescent hair, entirely incongruent with his lined thirty-something face, and looked at Janis. His hand rested on his wallet, which now sat on the bar top. She expected him to slide off the stool, but no, there was a glint of interest in his ocean blue eyes. She ought to shut up and return to her room. She looked away, only to find her gaze riveted on the glassy eyes of the decapitated buck. She looked back at the blue-eyed man.

"As it turns out, I'm an intelligent woman," she heard herself venture forth, "who's made some poor choices."

"I hear ya," the man said.

She reminded herself just then of the woman in Lessing's story, the cold calculation, the dry ice humor, strategizing. That wasn't her. She didn't fish for men. Especially not for this man, a good ten, maybe fifteen, years her junior. Yet, once she realized she had his attention, she looked away, pretended interest in the ancient photographs papering the tavern walls. Men in waders holding up ginormous fish. Men in plaid shirts grasping the opposing ends of a massive saw, the blade halfway through a thick evergreen tree trunk.

"Actually," she revised, "scratch that. I've made all the *right* choices, the ones you're supposed to make, and it's gotten me jack. Nada."

He grinned. Sucked up an ice cube from his empty Coke glass. "*Exactly.*"

Despite his hearty agreement, she bit back the urge to itemize the details: how she voted regularly, paid her bills on time, avoided unhealthy foods, and tried to make her marriage work. Her son and daughter were both independent and reasonably happy. Janis didn't know if she believed in God, but she had always believed in some kind of moral economy. Do bad, receive bad. Do good, receive good. Her mother had tried to warn her. In the end, that was probably the whole point in giving Janis the Lessing story, to spare her having to discover the meaninglessness of it all on her own.

"I left my husband this morning," she said. "You want to know the funny part?"

The man nodded.

"I checked into the Sea Breeze Motel." She cocked her head toward the south to indicate the shabby lodge next door to the bar. "And just to be, you know, ironic, I asked for room nineteen. The guy gave it to me!"

Now the blond man looked a bit alarmed.

"Oh, no suicides or anything like that are going to happen. I just need some time alone. Marianne Moore is this kickass poet, and she said that the cure for loneliness is solitude."

So why was she carrying on with a stranger in a seaside dive? She'd just told the dude that she was lonely, which is practically code for *fuck me*. Thoroughly humiliating because not only was that not what she meant, but she knew he was way out of her league, in the categories of both age and looks.

Thankfully the bartender finally arrived. The guy would pay and leave. She'd have her Marianne Moore solitude. But rather than paying for his Coke, he ordered another one. Janis heard herself ordering a hamburger and fries.

"My husband James thinks I'm too friendly," she said. "When he's being nice he says loquacious."

"You *are* chatty."

"We fought this morning because he threatened to pull the plug—those were his words—on my gallery."

Typically men were not good listeners, and so she ought to be suspicious of this guy. A voice of distrust, crouched inside her left temple, chanted, *Whoa, whoa, whoa.* She ignored this voice.

"He was mean. He said that pretty pictures don't pay bills. Which was his way of demeaning my art. I paint flowers, birds, ponds, okay? So what. I don't mind that my work isn't super original. People like it. I do sell paintings. But of course James is right, not enough to pay the heating bill."

Those blue eyes rested on her face. Okay, the man was listening. That didn't mean Janis needed to keep talking. Yet his attention made her feel as if doors in her chest were flying open. "The thing is, James's tiny metal sculptures would have sold, too—his shows got reviewed in *The Oregonian* and the *Willamette Weekly*—if he hadn't insisted on pricing them so high, taking himself so seriously." Janis sighed. "That's the saddest part, though. What I loved most about him, way back when, was the way he understood the value, the intrinsic value, of creating beautiful objects." She shook her head. "Of course he's right. We had two kids. We had to support them."

"But they're grown up now," the man said.

His understanding landed in her throat. She almost teared up as she said, "True."

"So," the man held up two palms, "it's obvious what's going on here."

Janis glanced around at the tattered photographs, the vinyl tabletops, the raw planking floor, the two dangling light bulbs. Then she realized he didn't mean here in the tavern, he meant the here of her own life.

The man said, "Your husband is bitter that he shut himself down."

"Exactly!"

"I don't know the dude, but no one should turn his back on his dream. If you do, you gotta take responsibility for that."

A familiar regret swamped Janis. Once again, she'd gone too far. Overshared. She shouldn't have criticized her husband to a stranger. She quickly checked to make sure the handful of old men and one middle-aged woman were still sitting dazed in the bar. She wasn't alone with the man. He was only drinking Coke. Still, she ought to leave. But he began talking about his own woes, and now she had to reciprocate, having blathered on about herself.

He talked about the repossession of his truck, the abandonment of a recent girlfriend. A heaviness, the murky load of someone else's nebulous problems, besieged her. "But guess what," he said, swirling his Coke glass in the wet puddle on the bar top.

He waited for Janis to say, "What?"

"My ship's come in. Literally."

He was handsome in a delayed kind of way. A little goofy with his blond messiness and too blue eyes, but his mouth had a firm set and his teeth were appealingly catawampus. His body—she shouldn't have looked—appeared to have done its fair share of work. He was no model but he looked lived in, a pair of favorite jeans. She still didn't know his name.

Her plate of food arrived, and Janis didn't count calories. She knifed up a generous glob of mayonnaise from the little white paper cup and spread it on the burger patty. She squeezed on a spiral of catsup. After capping the burger with the top bun, she took a big bite. It was delicious.

"Want a fry?"

He reached out a hand and it hovered, ever so briefly, over her plate, as if taking a fry sealed an agreement. That was ridiculous, of course, and he took and ate a fry.

He chugged a long drink of his Coke and slammed down the glass. "I'm a fourth generation fisherman. But the seas are fished out. We're not a dying breed, we're a dead one. My dad sold the boat, drank the proceeds, and then keeled. Heart attack at fifty-eight." He tapped his chest. "Your heart rebels if you don't follow it."

Hokey. But who was she to talk? She painted tulips and bird wings.

"I didn't take care of my grandma so she'd leave me the house," the man said. "I took care of her because she's my grandma. True, I needed somewhere to live. And yeah, she did leave me the house. Which I sold so I could get Elizabeth."

Janis tried to check her shock. She was talking to a strange man in a seaside tavern. She'd taken herself completely out of time. She didn't have any right to judge. At least mail-order brides entered into a clear economic transaction: I'll sleep in your bed (and of course service your body) and do your dishes and wash your clothes, and you'll provide the legal means and funds for American citizenship. She knew the bargain turned out badly for many women, but most probably knew the risks going in. Where was Elizabeth from? Uzbekistan? Cambodia?

"Do you love her?" Why not? Who was she to define the parameters of love?

"Oh!" He pounded his left breast. "Oh, yeah. Absolutely. She's perfect. Gorgeous."

"How long has she been here?"

"Not quite a month. There are a few loose ends to tie up, so I need to be a bit circumspect about where I keep her."

No doubt.

"I have her tied up at a public dock for the moment, but I have to keep moving her. Until I can afford a slip. And a license."

Janis nodded as if she'd known all along that *Elizabeth* was a boat, and maybe she had known, a little bit, but now she was disappointed.

The phone in his jeans pocket chirped.

"Hold on." He fished out the phone and smiled at her, as if she were an accomplice, as he quoted prices and recited a favorable weather report, which, she could tell, he was making up on the spot. He made arrangements to meet the caller at the public dock at six tomorrow morning and stuffed the phone back in his pocket. "Clients," he told Janis. "Gotta shove off. Nice to meet you. Good luck with . . . everything." He smiled a sunny, crooked, but super white-toothed smile, and shouted his goodbye to the bartender.

After he left, Janis paid her bill and crossed the street to stand facing the ocean. The big orange sun, aggressive in blasting its winter light, dropped into the sea. When the last bronze glimmer darkened to slate, she walked back to room nineteen in the Sea Breeze Motel. She locked the door and sat on the bed.

She'd wanted solitude. Here it was.

Well before dawn someone woke her up by pounding on the door. James! But no, he couldn't know where she'd gone because she used cash. The husband in "Room Nineteen" hired a detective, but Janis hadn't been gone long enough for that, and anyway, she didn't think James would bother. It had to be Fred, the motel proprietor. Maybe there was a fire? She imagined tall flames and their accompanying oxygen-swallowing *whoosh* devouring the bedclothes in the room next to hers. She sniffed for smoke, but smelled only the fetid carpeting.

Janis eased the ratty drapes back by an inch and viewed, standing before her door, the man from the tavern. She was appalled. What could he want? Perhaps after a night of drinking (she pictured him heading to another tavern after leaving the one where he met her and starting in on whisky), he'd decided he could overlook her notable seniority?

And what would be so bad about that? Susan, the protagonist in Lessings' story, had an affair in her famous motel room. The shock of the idea shimmered through Janis's whole body. Well, he didn't look like a criminal. Or even a lowlife. His family had been fishermen for four generations. He'd taken care of his grandma. He loved *Elizabeth* with all his heart. Janis let the drape fall and tiptoed to the door, her heart pounding. She pressed her palms against the greasy wood and breathed deeply, looking for the rules. They'd gone up in her imaginary fire. Janis unbolted and opened the door.

"Hey," the man said. "Sorry. I know it's early."

Early? It was still pitch dark. Janis had no idea if it was one o'clock or five o'clock.

"You're not, by any chance, looking for some quick cash, are you?"

He didn't lunge in the door. His tone was polite. The dull yellow porch light sorrowed the entreaty in his eyes. He was perhaps a bit desperate. She resisted the urge to reach up a hand and fluff her hair. She felt scandalous as she asked, "How much?"

He shuffled, swallowed, got that decidedly male buttressed look. "Fifty?"

The insult jarred back her senses. You couldn't buy a decent dinner out, not if you had wine, for fifty. Now she did fluff her hair, her thin aging hair. What an extraordinary moment: trying to decide her body's worth in dollars. She supposed hookers considered this math on a daily basis, but she'd never once thought about her own monetary worth in bed.

"I wouldn't walk your dog for fifty," she said and felt a lovely jolt of empowerment.

"Okay, seventy-five. Look, you'll be done by noon. It'll be easy."

Noon?

"Say yes. They're my first clients and I gotta look sharp. All you'll have to do is serve drinks and snacks. And chat. You're good at chatting. Think of yourself as a flight attendant. In first class."

She'd become the kind of woman who fabricated drama. James had said that, too, a few weeks ago, and he was right. Talk about desperate. A vicious grief ratcheted through her chest; she'd wanted this handsome fisherman to want her. Even if she didn't particularly want him. Janis looked over her shoulder at the thrown back bedcovers, the dark motel room, her desolation. "A hundred and fifty."

"I can't do that. I have about thirty in my pocket. It's all I have until the clients pay me. Come on, lady. Help me out here."

"My name is Janis."

He held out a big warm scratchy hand. "Ben. The clients are Suzanne and Elliott Spears. We can't let them know they're my first ever. They got my name from a friend who waits tables at the Pelican Inn, so you know, they're expecting a class act."

"A hundred." She always folded at the gallery when people

negotiated prices. She practically gave away most of her paintings. This new tough-as-nails feeling pleased her.

Ben hitched his whole body. "I'm making nothing, once I pay for gas. I already spent a fortune on the snacks and liquor."

Janis looked yet again at the bed where until half an hour ago she'd been sleeping alone, dreaming her usual fare of avalanches and tidal waves, mudslides and house fires. Maybe Marianne Moore was wrong.

"Look, I don't need you," Ben said starting to walk backwards. "I could do this by myself. But I'm trying to build the business. The Spears are clearly wealthy and therefore connected to other rich people. I'm willing to break even on this job if it brings me more clients. I kinda thought it might be a deal for you, too, but fine. I'm leaving."

"Wait."

He turned, opened his palms to the starry sky, exasperated.

"Plus half of any tips."

He hove a sigh and nodded.

Janis grabbed her purse, locked the door to room nineteen, and climbed into the cab of his truck. Moments later they pulled into the parking lot at the public dock. A breeze scuffled the surface of the harbor. *Elizabeth* was pretty with her crisp white hull and navy awning, rocking gently on her mooring, in the first tingle of morning light. Ben paused, resting his eyes on her as if she were indeed a woman, a lustful smile making him look goofy. "Grand Banks forty-five," he said. "I can't believe she's mine." He handed Janis a bag of groceries from Costco. "Go below. Get comfortable in the cabin. Start assembling the hors d'oeuvres." As she climbed aboard, he added, "Hey, Janis. Thank you."

She too fell in love with *Elizabeth* the moment she reached the bottom of the short ladder leading down to the tiny galley. Wasn't this all a person needed? A tidy ultra-functional kitchen and a body-sized bunk. She ran a hand along the couch, nestled under the kitchen table, and wondered how many people had made love on it.

Janis set the triangle of brie on a plate and put the Granny Smith apples next to a knife on the counter to cut up at the last minute, so the fruit wouldn't brown. She stowed the bottle of sauvignon blanc and the six-pack of local IPA beer in the tiny fridge, where she found already chilled bottles of vermouth and gin. She located the coffee maker and got a pot brewing. After arranging the apricot Danish pastries on a plate, she wadded up and hid the Costco packaging, evidence of the food's provenance, in the bottom of the garbage pail.

As she climbed back up to the deck, she felt as if she were stepping into the pinking sky. A ridiculous elation lit her like dawn. She had no business feeling happy about leaving her marriage, going to sea with a strange man, taking a job as a boat steward, and yet she was delighted. She handed Ben a fresh cup of coffee.

"Showtime," he said, nodding toward the parking lot where a silver BMW slunk to a stop. Elliott and Suzanne Spears emerged from the padded interior. Already the sky had deepened to orange over the land and a shimmering pale blue over the sea.

"Good morning!" Ben boomed. He hopped off the boat and strode up the pier with a hearty hand extended. The Spears wore matching expensive red parkas with fur trim, as if they were heading for the Antarctic. After shaking their hands, Ben rubbed his vigorously. "Boy, do we have a morning lined up for you!"

Janis dropped below to zap the apricot Danish pastries in the microwave. She poured two cups of coffee and climbed back as the couple boarded the boat. "Hi, I'm Ben's wife, Janis. Sugar? Cream?"

"Yes," Suzanne said.

"Black," Elliott said.

Ben, still on the dock behind the clients, guffawed silently, raised his hands in a WTF gesture, but smiled.

Next she brought up the tray of Danish. "From our local bakery. Another husband-wife team. Every single ingredient is local-sourced. They have their own cow and churn their own butter. They even have their own micro orchard. They grew these apricots."

Suzanne took a big bite. "Oh, I can tell. Delicious." She unzipped her expedition parka to reveal a fawn-colored cashmere sweater.

"Do we have to go out far before we see the whales?" Elliott asked.

Ben opened his mouth, but Janis jumped in with, "A little distance, yes. But oh my, yesterday they were flip-flopping all around us. We saw upwards of a dozen."

Elliott gave a hard little nod, as if agreeing to a business transaction, and then pretended to be joking as he tossed out, "Money back if we don't see any, right?"

Ben laughed nervously.

"Oh, we'll see them," Janis said. No wonder she hadn't spied any fishing gear on board. They were going whale watching! What an adventure! The sun shouted its agreement, rising above the Douglas firs, and the breeze had died. The sea sighed calm and flat, a perfect winter day. All Janis had to do was keep the Spears happy.

As they putted out of the harbor, she refilled their coffee cups, made up gracious answers to their questions, and even found a pair of visors when the couple complained of the sun's angle. Once they were settled on the deck benches, Elliott with his enormous telephoto lens resting along his leg, she went to stand by Ben at the helm. She put an arm around his waist and her head on his shoulder. He grinned at her and even kissed her forehead; he approved of the story she'd created for the day. They were an honest, hardworking Oregon coast couple whose family had been fishing from the Pacific for generations. They came from enterprising stock and knew how to work the changing economy. It was a narrative that comforted the Spears because it cast them as helpers. And one that stirred Janis. Perhaps the cure to loneliness was becoming a different person. The day glittered with optimism.

Indeed, a moment later, Ben's back hitched with pleasure. He calmed the motor, made his face grave, as if informed by an ancient understanding, as he squinted westward and nodded slowly.

Coffee sloshed out of Elliott's cup as he slammed it down and leapt to his feet. "Where?" he shouted.

"About halfway to the horizon."

Janis still had her arm around Ben's waist and she could feel the relief in his body. Not even half an hour out. She saw the disturbance on the surface of the sea and helped the Spears see it, too.

Just as Suzanne said, "That's all?" a sleek dark back rounded out of the water, rolling forward. The whale submerged and then surfaced again. A classic spout, high and sparkling, sprayed against the blue sky. A second whale, a baby, emerged and slid alongside its mother's huge slick body.

"A female gray and her calf, migrating south." Ben used a deep tour guide voice.

The Spears laughed out loud, and both of their faces looked genuinely joyful. Elliott planted the camera with its long telephoto lens against his face. Ben steered the boat in the direction of the whales and Janis went below. She quickly cut up the Granny Smith apples, which she decided were also from the baker couple's orchard, and arranged the slices around the brie, which was oozing nicely out of its triangle shape.

As she brought up the tray, Suzanne was saying, "This calls for a celebration, I should think."

"Absolutely!" Ben rallied. "Beer? Wine? A martini?"

"A martini! Heavens!" Suzanne sang out, as if an alcoholic beverage hadn't occurred to her but now that he'd suggested it, "Why not!"

Janis dropped down to make the drink. She popped open a beer for Elliott, too, though he hadn't asked for one. As she delivered the drinks, she ballyhooed, "You're super lucky! A calf, a spout, two whales!"

"You saw a dozen yesterday," Elliott pointed out. "Will we see blues?"

"Where'd they go?" Suzanne asked.

"They're whales," Janis said, suddenly annoyed by the couple's insatiability. "They swim underwater."

Ben shot her a warning look.

Right: rich people, flight attendant. An attitude lapse was not allowed.

Elliott chugged some beer and said, "We'll see more, won't we?"

"Oh, yeah." Ben sped up, chasing the horizon, though the mother and calf pair had disappeared.

A bit of wind kicked up, scuffing the surface of the water. Frothy whitecaps jiggled the boat. Elliott sat back down, looking a bit green about the gills. Janis turned her face to the sun and enjoyed the cold spray stinging her face. She'd do her best, but it wasn't like Ben could fire her. She'd torn her life down the middle, and look what she found behind the sheet of it! Sunshine, ocean spray, whales, an entirely new story.

Elliott groaned, spread his knees, and vomited between his legs, right onto the deck.

Suzanne sprang away from him and scowled at Janis, as if she'd been the one to barf.

Her happy moment killed, Janis went below to find rags. It took several moppings and towel-rinsings, not to mention suppressed gaggings, before she had the deck clean, and then Suzanne wanted another martini. As she balanced the cocktail glass on her way back up to the deck, Janis heard the whine of another motor. A small and dilapidated skiff, its bow flying off the surface of the water, headed straight for the *Elizabeth*. A bearded man sat at the stern, hand on the throttle, and a ruddy youth sat amidships. Ben accelerated abruptly and some of Suzanne's martini splashed out of the glass.

"Shit!" she cried and tossed back what was left before more was lost.

Elliott gripped the deck railing, looking as if he might hurl again, and began to shout, "What's going on? Hey! What is this?"

The skiff roared closer, nimble on the water compared to the much larger *Elizabeth*.

Suzanne waved her martini glass at Janis, who ignored her. No way would she go below when pirates were about to overtake them.

She thought she was making fun of herself, her penchant for drama, using the word pirates, when the skiff pulled alongside them and the fresh-faced adolescent drew a gun and pointed it at her. Janis's knees jellied and her throat constricted.

Suzanne screamed.

Ben shouted, "Whoa!" and killed the engine. The skiff idled up against the *Elizabeth*. "What the fuck?" Ben shouted. "Put that down!"

"Easiest way to do this," said the bearded man, "is a straightforward trade. You folks come on board the *Lusty Lady* and we take the *Elizabeth*. No one gets hurt. End of deal."

Elliott gripped the deck railing and drew big breaths, as if his first priority was keeping down his Danish and beer. Suzanne hyperventilated, emitting rodent-like squeaks.

Ben reached for the intercom, just under the wheel, and the bearded guy guffawed a big forced laugh. "I wouldn't do that, I were you."

Ben hesitated.

"*Do it,*" Suzanne trilled. "For Christ sake, call the fucking police."

The kid with a gun nodded at the dropped martini glass. "Make me one of those."

"Don't be an idiot," the bearded guy said to the boy. "Just get them in the skiff."

"Check it out!" The kid's excited voice cracked. "This is an opportunity. Look at the rock on her finger. The guy's camera. We're going out of the reach of the law anyway, so why not take the dude for a quick trip to the bank. Fast cash. Drop them all in some cove on our way to China."

"Stick to the plan, son. We're taking the boat."

"The plan just got better!" The kid spoke as if he were suggesting a strategy for a day at the zoo rather than grand larceny.

"You're not doing this," Ben said, his voice quavering with rage.

"Yeah, actually we are."

"You're gonna get caught and go to prison."

Ben was strangely relaxed. His tone of voice suggested familiarity. He knew these guys.

"Give me the gun," the guy with the beard said to the boy, who reluctantly turned it over. The older man pointed it at Suzanne. "You, the lady with the face job. Jump on board."

Suzanne impressed Janis by saying, "No fucking way."

The kid launched himself at the *Elizabeth*'s deck railing, grabbed it with both hands, and boarded the bigger vessel. He wrapped an oversized adolescent hand around Suzanne's upper arm and started dragging her to the starboard railing. "Chicks don't talk back to my dad."

"Easy there," said the bearded guy. He tried to keep the gun pointed at Suzanne, but the sea rolled under the little skiff, rocking his stance, making the arm holding the gun rotate in circles. He said, "Ben, this can be easy or difficult, your choice."

Shock dropped Janis onto a deck bench; they *did* know him.

"Get off my boat," Ben said to the kid.

"Not your boat, dude." With that the bearded man shoved the gun in the waistband of his jeans and began to hoist himself on board, too. Ben lunged, shoulder first, and attempted to shove the man away from the deck railing. But the bearded man had the momentum, and Ben bounced off the burliness and fell onto his own deck. He sprawled on his back, arms and legs in the air, like a toppled insect. The intruder retrieved his gun, glanced around at the *Elizabeth* passengers, and chose Janis. He placed the nozzle against her temple and said, "Justin, get everyone's phones."

Janis's thoughts were a scalding soup of people and places. She'd made a mistake. She loved James with all her heart. She loved her children even more. Her bed, just her bed, had gone underappreciated for years. Her insides were churning, her head exploding, with the cold circle of metal against her temple.

The boy shoved his hand into everyone's pockets and retrieved their phones. Three went flying to their graves in the Pacific, but he held onto Elliott's, his thumb navigating the screen.

"Toss it," the bearded man said.

"It's a seven, Dad! Anyway, maybe I can get into his bank account real simple, right here. A quick transfer."

"Toss it. Now."

Justin moaned, arched his thin torso as he drew back his arm and threw the phone out to sea, shouting, "Hee haw!"

"You'll go to prison, Daniel," Ben repeated, gravel in his voice.

"I don't think so. You have no recourse. The *Elizabeth* isn't registered. You're operating a business without a license. You can't afford the fines. Either they take the boat or I do."

"We'll prosecute to the fullest extent of the law," Suzanne said. The martini and a half had served her well; she was more relaxed than anyone else.

"Maybe you should keep your mouth shut," Elliott suggested.

"Is that any way to talk to your wife?" Daniel swung the gun around and pointed it at Elliott.

Janis collapsed onto the bench, the relief instant and overwhelming. And yet, in its wake a quivering arousal buzzed through her. *Pirates!*

"I gave you a chance to do the right thing," Daniel said to Ben in almost a whine. "You didn't. You got greedy. So, game on, the *Elizabeth* is now mine." Then, perhaps embarrassed by the emotion in his voice, he added a hardened, "Asshole."

"*I'm* the one who took care of Grandma."

"Oh, yeah, for a whole, what, two months? That gives you the right to sell her house and keep every penny of the proceeds? I think not. Besides, you 'took care of Grandma'"—Daniel made air quotes—"because you were fucking homeless is why. Nice try, brother, but you're a common greed-wad."

"Grandma would be disgusted with you," Ben spat.

"Grandma is dead." Daniel gestured with the gun toward the

starboard side of the Grand Banks. "Get your clients on board the *Lusty Lady*. Lickety-split."

"It's not seaworthy," Ben said.

Janis looked out at the vast stretch of the Pacific Ocean, considering the possibility of her imminent death, sinking in the rusty little skiff, which made her hyperaware of her tender life. This overwhelming feeling of being alive blotted out her hearing and sight. She wallowed in her soft animal body wanting only to live.

Until Daniel's words, "You idiot!" broke through her biological trance. He now waved the gun at the kid. "You fucking didn't tie her off?"

Ben, Daniel, and Justin looked over the side of the *Elizabeth* and Janis understood that the *Lusty Lady* had drifted away.

There she was, a good two hundred yards off, riding a current that quickly opened the gap between the two boats.

Daniel's anger fizzled and now he laughed. "Ben's right. It's a piece of junk. Not made for the sea in the first place. We can put them off in Pebble Cove. That'll hold 'em a lot longer, anyway. Give us more time."

As Daniel and Justin high-fived, Ben made a bid for the gun in his brother's other hand. He managed to knock it to the deck of the boat, but Daniel kicked it away. Elliott sprang, wrapped his hand around the handle, but Justin socked him in the face and picked up the dropped gun.

"Hey, easy now," Daniel said, scowling at his son's violence. He turned to Ben. "Look. This is a good deal for you, bro. You'll go scot-free." He laughed again. "Eventually. No one needs to know you were trying to operate a business and a boat without licenses. That you were trying to swindle these nice folks."

Ben glanced at his client, who now had blood streaming down his cheek, and then back at his brother. He started nodding at Daniel's narrative, undoubtedly seeing the advantages in it for himself, and Janis thought she too might prefer a cove over bobbing about in the decidedly not seaworthy *Lusty Lady*.

Justin now had the gun, which made the situation decidedly more volatile than when Daniel controlled the weapon, and Janis watched with relief as Ben made his way to the wheel. No one spoke a word as he drove the *Elizabeth* around two small headlands. The whole while Justin alternated among his victims, giving everyone a turn at looking down the short barrel of that gun.

When the gun was pointed at her, Janis's brain quivered like a jellyfish and she had no thoughts at all. When it pivoted away, she worried about the cove. Would there be crashing waves? Wet barnacle-crusted boulders? How about an incoming tide?

When they finally entered the cove, she did notice, briefly and remotely, as if her thoughts were on a screen outside her own head, that the spot was quite pretty. The cove was protected by rocky headlands and backed by a steep cliff. The beach itself was pebbled and sunny, and two haystack rocks stood guard just outside the surf. Janis entertained survival fantasies: sharpening sticks to spear fish; building a shelter out of driftwood and rocks; drinking from the trickle of water sluicing down the cliff. Ben eased the *Elizabeth* as far into the cove as he dared.

"Why can't we keep the old guy?" the kid asked. "Quick cash. If he refuses, we kill the wife."

"That might be incentive to refuse," Daniel said. "Everyone off the boat."

"There's no dingy," Ben said dully.

"Then I hope everyone can swim."

Elliott and Suzanne Spears remained silent as Ben handed out life jackets. Then he went first, climbing down the ladder on the side of the hull. Janis decided she was going next, sticking as close to Ben as possible, although she'd lost all belief in his safety or innocence. When she splashed off the last rung of the ladder into the sea, the cold knocked her breath away. She kicked hard and wheeled her arms in a chaotic swim, making the shore in just a few seconds. She crawled out on the pebbled beach like some evolutionary creature.

The sun's warmth made her clothes steam instantly, and she sat there, breathing in life, and watched the Spears thrash their way toward shore. Elliott had an arm around Suzanne's chest, and he heroically towed her in.

Daniel and Justin, who waited to make sure everyone survived the swim, waved before navigating the *Elizabeth* out of the cove and onward toward, for all she knew, the South Sea.

The marooned crew spread out on the beach, each to his or her own stone, to dry in the thankfully bright sun. Ben asked if anyone had matches, so he could build a fire, but no one even answered him.

"I'm sorry," Ben called over to Janis. "You seem like a nice lady."

"You're not even his wife," Suzanne said. "Oh, are you two both in huge trouble."

Janis rose from her rock and strode to the base of the cliff. She looked up the slope made of loose soil, beach grass, and a patch of spruce and hemlock on the higher reaches. The angle of the cliff was at least sixty degrees, probably steeper. She imagined what would happen if she tried to scale it and failed: the muddy tumble to her death, her body crashing onto the stones at the bottom of the cliff.

Oh, she wanted to go home.

She used her hands like claws, trying to hold onto the crumbling soil, as she kicked in steps. She didn't look down, just moved upward, her feet hitching onto embedded stones, only to have them slide away. The clumps of beach grass held better, and she moved from one of these to the next, like a rock climber searching out handholds. Sweat streamed down her face, neck, and back. Her lungs burned with their effort to process more oxygen faster. She was a crab, a badger, an elk as she climbed. Even a cloud, floating to the next secure place. Time became cellular, a matter of her body's ability, and she had no idea, if someone had been looking at a watch, how long it took her to reach the pithy soil under the first spruce. Her perception of safety was illusory, though, because those evergreen droppings were more slippery than the soil. She slid a good ten feet before she was able to dig in her toes to stop her fall. When she regained the area under the spruce, she carefully dug out steps until she got to its trunk, which she hugged, her cheek against a drip of pitch.

From there the climb was easier. She could move from one tree trunk to the next, positioning herself so that if she plunged, she'd run into and be stopped by one of the spruces.

Janis stood on top of the cliff, covered with mud, heaving with the effort of hard breathing, and gazed down at the beach. Suzanne was screaming at Ben, and he was holding her by the wrists. Elliott stood at a distance, looking out to sea, as if for a rescue boat, apparently uninterested in his wife's skirmish with Ben.

"People," Janis said out loud, "are nuts."

Ben let go of Suzanne and lunged for the muddy cliff. He began climbing. Janis felt a ridiculous little spurt of cheer at seeing him attempt an escape. After all, no one would die. Ben, or maybe even she, could anonymously call the Coast Guard. The Spears would be rescued.

Janis looked beyond the cove, out at the glittering sea, and there the backs of three gray whales humped out of the water. A migrating pod. Were they lonely, too? In spite of their epic swim? The mouthfuls of fish and shrimp they swallowed? The young ones they lifted with their backs and fins to the air for breathing?

It was anyone's guess how far she'd have to walk before she came to a road, before she found a way off this coastal headland. But looking inland she could see farms and even towns in the distance, so she'd get somewhere, sooner or later. Of course she'd return home to James. After all, it wasn't the first time she'd taken a sabbatical from him. She may or may not close her gallery. Life would go on. With its devastating disappointments. Its small joys. The occasional ecstasy.

Too Big for My Britches

Sarah Kotchian

When britches were breeches,
ladies side-saddled, didn't
straddle the steed,
never galloped, indeed,

we pulled in our reins,
learned to mind p's and q's
am I taking up space?
if I am, please excuse,

I suggest, if I may,
asked permission, forgiveness,
kept our vanity, chastity,
viewpoints in place.

Now it's orange and purple,
colors jostle for loudness
together declare
my presence is here

I want baggy, expansive
folds that are ample
I claim my abundance,
take up space in the room

My clothing now fits,
when I breathe, it moves with me
if I had any cleavage
there'd be room for that, too

no need of belts
or to hide my behind
I have life left to live
and some growing to come

I've had it with habits,
the meekness of rabbits,
got too big for my britches—

so now I wear none.

Boxes That Won't Fit

Heather Anderson

Look at me.
Or not.

Today I declare my independence.
I step from the box that I shut myself in.
I don't want to play this game of winners
and losers anymore—
won't wait for you to pick me for your team,
won't stare at the ground hoping
I will fit into your
just like me
thinks like me
can mold into me
will follow me
box.

I am made from numberless mountains
crushed over uncounted millions of years
into fine dust mixed with green leaves
turned red
turned brown and
ground down by uncounted feet
just for the joy of the sound,

churned together in a downpour of
raindrops and thundered yawps,
reeled past in torrents of melting snow
accumulated over long winter months
molecule by
molecule,
swirled around in eddies and spit
out of the mud.
You cannot put me in your box
because I will not fit.

As you sit in your white,
self-made, four-walled shrine to
immortality, moving your acolytes
around your game board,
the walls are crumbling around you.
The cast-offs you throw out the window
are fizzing and popping,
growing the detritus into innumerable
new mountains.

This is my immortality—
I raise my head and look at you.

You cannot put me in your box.

Dust and Blood

Janet Ruth

I.
West of the river
I watch the desert dance—
      tawny, sun-burnt,
      clad in shades of dust and blood.
She shimmers among the heat waves,
shares with me the prickly blanket
of cactus and cholla, rattlesnake and scorpion,
that drapes across her scarred and wrinkled skin,
her bones, her secret, sacred parts.

Here, upon the plateaus
that rise above the Río Grande's rift,
I dance with the desert—
      with coyote and roadrunner,
      kangaroo rat and tarantula—
as dust devils twist
into the bleached sky
and sand sage rolls in waves.
My eyes turn west.
How does the desert dance below Mount Taylor?
Or does she sing to Tsoodzil—Turquoise Mountain—
that sacred corner of the Navajo world?

The desert—goddess of sand,
sun and blistering wind—
slows her dance, lets go my hand.
On the rim of a red rock mesa,
      her sinewy legs of twisted juniper
      planted firmly among the rocky rubble of ages,
she burns a smudge stick of pungent sage.
Its smoke wafts toward the mountain,
elicits volcanic dreams, memories of lava
flowing scarlet and hot as blood—
now clotted, crumbly and black.
Beneath her bloody dreams
the desert and I lay ourselves down
in the shrinking, speckled shade
of a gnarled desert hackberry
to wait.

II.
At dusk, I feel that gritty goddess turn,
gaze east toward the Sandías Mountains—
      sprawled beyond the Río Grande,
      watermelon-red in the setting sun.
A cry twists among the peaks.
Perhaps it is Wankwijo—
the Pueblo peoples' Old Wind Woman.
Below the Sandías, the great, shallow river flows,
mirrors a darkening sky—
      starry embers of an ancient, banked fire
      are lifted to flames in its reflection.
Beneath the blazing heavens—the wind crone's wail.
The mountains tremble,
the desert smiles,

I hold my breath.
Old Wind Woman moans,
parts her bony knees—

births the full moon.

Contributors

COURI JOHNSON is a graduate of the Northeast Ohio Master of Fine Arts, currently attending the University of Louisiana at Lafayette for a PhD in creative writing. She works with fairytale motifs and primarily writes fabulism, but sometimes plays with horror as well. Her short story collection, *I'll Tell You a Love Story*, is available through Bridge Eight Press. For more of her work check www.courijohnson.com.

JUDE RITTENHOUSE received a Writer's Grant from the Vermont Studio Center and poetry awards from Glimmer Train Press, Inc., and Poets and Patrons of Chicago. Her poems have been published in *Nimrod International Journal, Tiferet Journal, DoveTales, Newport Review*, and *Lay Bare the Canvas: New England Poets on Art*, among others. A founding coeditor of the feminist literary magazine *Moon Journal* (1995–2009, archived in the Sophia Smith Collection at Smith College), she has taught writing and inner-growth classes and been a speaker at conferences, retreats, schools, hospitals, hospices, and domestic violence shelters for thirty years. With a master's degree in counseling, along with extensive additional training, she is in private practice in Rhode Island. See more at www.JudeRittenhouse.com.

HANNAH YANG is a speculative fiction writer living in Colorado. She loves black coffee, watercolor painting, and stories of all kinds. Find her on Twitter at @hannahxyang.

As a student at Sweet Briar College in Virginia, **BRODERICK EATON** studied with poet Mary Oliver and author John Gregory Brown. Her poetry has appeared in numerous publications, including *Crosswinds Poetry Journal, Smartish Pace, Writer's Digest, Flying South, Verseweavers,* and *The Source Weekly.* She won first place for new poets in the Oregon Poetry Association contest, followed shortly by the Sixfold Poetry Prize. Her poems have also recently been named runner-up for the Erskine J. Poetry Prize, and finalist for both the 49th Parallel Award and the Tucson Festival of Books poetry award. Her short fiction has been a finalist for the New Millennium Prize and appeared as an honorable mention entry in the *Stories That Need to Be Told* anthology. She is nearing the finish line for an MFA through Lindenwood University and has a chapbook coming out in 2022 with Finishing Line Press. She lives with her family in the high desert of Oregon.

KRISTINA VAN SANT has published poems in *Atlanta Review, Journal of New Jersey Poets, Talking River Review,* and elsewhere, and has work forthcoming in Slippery Elm. Born and raised in southern New Jersey, she moved to New York to attend the graduate writing program at Sarah Lawrence College, where she obtained her MFA. She now lives in central New Jersey, and is currently employed as a grant writer at a nonprofit zoological society.

ELLEN PAULEY GOFF is a graduate from the University of Chicago with a BA in English language and literature, film studies, and creative writing. Her short fiction has been published in the *Indiana Review* and *Hunger Mountain,* and was chosen as a finalist in Glimmer Train's Fiction Open contest. Her work has been named a winner of the San Francisco Writers Conference Writing Contest as well as the Vermont College of Fine Arts' Katherine Paterson Prize for Young Adult and Children's Writing, and she is also the inaugural recipient of SCBWI's A. Orr Fantasy Grant for children's speculative fiction. Ellen was born and raised in Kentucky, but now lives in New York City, where she founded and leads Underground

YA, a YA-focused writing workshop and critique group whose mission includes providing publishing knowledge and resources to unagented, unpublished, and traditionally excluded writers.

BROOKE HERTER JAMES is the author of two poetry chapbooks, *The Widest Eye* and *Spring Took the Long Way Around*, one prose poetry/photography collection, *Postcards from Montana*, and one children's book, *Why Did the Farmer Cross the Road?* Her poems have appeared in *PoemTown Vermont, Mountain Troubadour Poetry Journal, Orbis,* and *Rattle,* as well as the online publications *Poets Reading the News, New Verse News, Flapper Press, Typishly,* and *Writing in a Woman's Voice.* She was chosen as a finalist in the Poetry Society of Vermont's 2019 National Poetry Contest. She lives on a small farm in Vermont with her husband, four hens, two donkeys, and a dog.

LILA QUINN is a poet from rural Missouri. After studying at Webster University from 2008 to 2012 under the guidance of her friend and mentor the late Missouri poet laureate David Clewell, she earned her MFA from the University of Wisconsin–Madison in 2015. She later studied meditation in residence at an ashram for sixteen months. Lila considers writing her lifelong calling. Poetry, when it arrived, was not just a survival raft, it became her sturdy ship for coming home to herself. She now lives in Boulder, Colorado.

MELLISA PASCALE is a writer and graduate student in the MA nonfiction writing program at Johns Hopkins University. Her work has been published by *Passion Passport, Matador Network, Go Overseas,* and *Business Travel Life.* Presently, she is working on a memoir about her eleven-month backpacking trip in New Zealand and Japan.

MAHALIA SOLAGES' fiction has appeared *Kalyani Magazine,* Momaya Press, Almond Press, a trilingual anthology *So Spoke the Earth, Writing Raw,* and Writers Retreat, Principus Studios. Also a playwright, her play, *A Tale of Two Mommies* was featured in Miami at the Centro Cultural de

Espana. She has authored two children's picture books. When she isn't writing short stories, she has a blog, *SHow-UP-DIfferently* (SHUDI), and co-hosts at *Badass Black Girl*. She lives in Fort Lauderdale.

SUE STORTS is a retired child, adolescent, and adult psychiatrist who lives in Tulsa, Oklahoma. She writes poetry, short stories, middle grade, and young adult fiction.

KIPLING KNOX is an author, illustrator, and conservationist with roots in Illinois and Washington state. He's currently at work on a collection of stories called *Ghosts of the New World*. He has written stories and scripts for full-scale video games and placed twice in the annual Epic Writers contest of Puget Sound. You can find samples of his work at kiplingknox.com.

BECKY JENSEN is a writer and podcast contributor who lives in a little cabin on a wild river in Northern Colorado. Her writing has appeared in *Misadventures*, on *Out There* podcast, and in *Rise*, winner of the 2020 Colorado Book Award. She's author of two stories in *The Road She's Traveled*, a forthcoming anthology that profiles the remarkable strength and resilience of ordinary women. When not on assignment, she's writing a memoir about running away from home, and into the mountains for five weeks, when she was forty-five. You can find her at beckyjensenwrites.com.

JACQUELINE SHEEHAN, PhD, is a bestselling novelist. She also publishes essays in the *New York Times* (Modern Love), *The Writer*, and *Edible Pioneer Valley*. She was a commentator on Public Radio in Western Massachusetts and Albany, NY. Her novels include *The Comet's Tale*, based on the life of Sojourner Truth, *Lost & Found*, *Now & Then*, *Picture This*, *The Center of the World*, and *The Tiger in the House*. Her books have been translated into eight languages. She was awarded fellowships at Hawthornden Castle in Scotland and Jentel Arts in Wyoming, and

Turkey Land Cove on Martha's Vineyard. Jacqueline is one of the founders and past president of Straw Dog Writers Guild in Massachusetts. She teaches writing workshops in Massachusetts and at international retreats. See more at www.jacquelinesheehan.com.

NORA BONNER's stories have appeared in various journals and anthologies including *Shenandoah*, the *North American Review*, the *Bellingham Review*, the *Indiana Review*, the *Potomac Review*, *Hobart*, *Quarterly West*, *Redivider*, and *Best American Non-Required Reading*. She writes and teaches in Atlanta, Georgia, where she recently earned a PhD in creative writing from Georgia State University. She also works as a program coordinator for higher ed in a prison program at Lee Arrendale State Prison, a maximum security facility for women in Alto, Georgia. She is originally from Detroit.

PETER YOUNG . . .

- is a twin. Both his parents were artists.
- He has lived in 31 places and had 115 roommates over the years.
- A bear turned and roared at him while he was bicycle touring high up in the Cascade Mountains of Oregon.
- For a year, he voluntarily lived and worked in a 220-person women's shelter in Washington, DC. He was the first man ever on staff.
- He once scored 16 points in a quarter playing for the Willamette Wildcat's eighth-grade basketball team.
- He has never owned a car. Once he rode his bicycle to Alaska.
- He's done six years of counseling and still needs tune-ups now and then.
- Once, beside a mountain lake at dusk, he heard a bat sneeze as it flew by him.
- When a gun was pulled on him while hitchhiking across Nova Scotia he defused the situation by talking.
- He's had 43 different jobs. Presently he's a life skills coach for people with special needs.
- He lives in Vancouver, WA, with his amazing wife, who is a kick-ass social worker. A Black Lives Matter flag hangs outside their front door.

ANNE MORALES is an artist from Oklahoma City. Her love of stories and the written word comes from her mom, Sharon. She lives at home with her husband Gabriel and their two daughters. She also has the pleasure of living with two goofy dogs, a shady old cat, and a feisty little cat who named herself queen of the neighborhood.

NAN JACKSON is a poet and writer living in East Lansing, Michigan. Her poetry has appeared in anthologies of the Peninsula Writers and her nonfiction in *The Sun* (Readers Write) and *Pulse: Voices from the Heart of Medicine* (More Voices). Her poem "Shiawassee Street Bridge" is engraved in the pavement along the River Trail in downtown Lansing. Nan's adventures in recent years include travels far and wide with her husband, Vern Mesler, related to their work in the preservation of historic iron and steel bridges. During three years teaching mathematics at a K–12 school in the Caribbean, Nan was a frequent scuba diver who almost always followed rigorous safety protocols as she explored the awe-inspiring worlds under water.

MARY KATE WILCOX is an author from Overland Park, Kansas. Her nonfiction essay "My Birds" appeared in *34th Parallel Magazine*. She won the 2021 Overall Prose Award in the Kansas Voices Writing Contest and the first place short story award for her work "Untethered." She completed two years at Kansas State University studying conservation biology and currently works at a dog boarding facility. Mary Kate spends most of her free time birding, kayaking, hiking, and writing.

GENÉT BOSQUÉ—poet, fiction writer, performer—is editing her second volume of poems, *She Who Leaps*, and completing a first novel, *Decipher Her Eyes*. Her poems appear in the *California Quarterly*, *Hard Pressed*, *Synapse*, and *Towards a Feminist Consideration of Language*. As an artist-in-residence, she's led poetry and performance workshops at mental health centers, for people with AIDS, for at-risk and LGBTQ+ teens—she edited/published nine anthologies of their work, and directed/

produced two solo performance shows. She believes fiercely in poetry as oral literature—and loves to give readings! She has an MA in cultural anthropology (comparative religions/ethnopoetry). *NOTE: Takanakapsaluk is a Northwest Coast tribe goddess of sea creatures who lives at the bottom of the ocean—with long, tangled hair.*

Australian storyteller, author, poet, and Steiner/Waldorf teacher, MELISSA MIN is a committed educator with a passion for bringing the creative arts to community spaces. She is particularly dedicated to preserving rare artistic and creative processes that are at risk of falling into obscurity. Melissa is founder of Circa—Storytelling Workshops for Wellbeing and runs groups, workshops, and sacred Storytelling Circles in Perth, Western Australia.

RED HAWK is the author of ten books of poetry: *Journey of the Medicine Man* (August House, 1983), *The Sioux Dog Dance* (Cleveland State University, 1991), *The Way of Power* (Hohm Press, 1996), *The Art of Dying* (Hohm Press, 1999), *Wreckage with a Beating Heart* (Hohm Press, 2005), *Raven's Paradise* (Bright Hill Press Poetry Prize, 2010), *Mother Guru* (Hohm Press, 2014), *Return to the Mother* (Hohm Press, 2017), *The Way of the Wise Woman* (Hohm Press, 2019), and *The Law of the Land* (Aubade Press, 2020), as well as two nonfiction books: *Self Observation: The Awakening of Conscience* (Hohm Press, 2009) and *Self Remembering: The Path to Non-Judgmental Love* (Hohm Press, 2015). Red Hawk is an Earth name, received during a four-day water fast at the Buffalo River, in the dead of winter during the worst ice storm Arkansas had seen in many years. It was given by our Mother Earth, bought as answered prayer, paid for by enduring suffering. It is not an Indian name.

LUCY JANE BLEDSOE is the author of eight books of fiction, including *The Evolution of Love, Lava Falls,* and *A Thin Bright Line,* which the *New York Times* said "triumphs as an intimate and humane evocation of day-to-day life under inhumane circumstances." Her fiction has won a

California Arts Council Fellowship in Literature, an American Library Association Stonewall Award, the Arts & Letters Fiction Prize, a Pushcart nomination, a Yaddo Fellowship, and two National Science Foundation Artists & Writers Fellowships. Bledsoe was raised by wolves.

SARAH KOTCHIAN's book *Camino* about her 500-mile solo pilgrimage in Spain received the New Mexico and Arizona Book Award and Seven Sisters Book Award. Her writing has appeared in *Tiny Seed Literary Journal, Persimmon Tree, Bosque Journal, Listen, Presence,* and *ABQ inPrint,* and the Podcast *The Unruly Muse.* She was a contributor in poetry at the 2019 Bread Loaf Writers' Conference. Retired from a career in environmental health, she finds much inspiration for her writing from the wild lands around her home in New Mexico.

HEATHER ANDERSON is a former environmental lawyer living in New Mexico. She spent several years volunteering as a sustainability and gardening merit badge counselor for the Boy Scouts of America and for Catholic Charities helping refugees. Heather is currently writing and teaching herself to paint while helping her four boys navigate online school and the COVID pandemic.

JANET RUTH is a New Mexico ornithologist. Her writing focuses on connections to the natural world. She has recent poems in *Tiny Seed Literary Journal, Sin Fronteras, Spiral Orb, Unlost: Journal of Found Poetry & Art,* and anthologies including *Moving Images: Poetry Inspired by Film* (Before Your Quiet Eyes Publications, 2021) and *New Mexico Remembers 9/11* (Artemesia Publishing, 2020). Her first book, *Feathered Dreams: celebrating birds in poems, stories & images* (Mercury HeartLink, 2018) was a finalist for the 2018 NM/AZ Book Awards. See more at redstartsandravens.com/janets-poetry.

Made in the USA
Columbia, SC
02 March 2023

13184256R00113